# stress management

To: the love of my life!!!

May this book assist you w/ your new healthy life in 2006.

love me, xxoo

# stress management

Jane Collingwood

MQP

## Caution

If you are pregnant, have given birth in the last six weeks, or have a medical condition, such as high blood pressure, spinal problems, arthritis, or asthma, consult your medical practitioner or an experienced teacher before starting any exercise.

## About the author

JANE COLLINGWOOD is a freelance writer who regularly contributes to magazines such as *International Health Care Journal* and *Stressfree Living* and provides health news for several medical websites. She has a BSc in Psychology, and an MSc in The Psychology of Health. Having worked in the NHS and other medical institutions, she has substantial knowledge of health and psychology and believes passionately in getting information and ideas across to a wider audience. Jane lives in Bristol with her husband, Dave.

## Picture credits

p.15 © Mehau Kulyk/Science Photo Library; pp.10, 82 © Tom Stewart/CORBIS: p.23 © LWA-Dann Tardif/CORBIS; pp.27, 103 © Jose Luis Pelaez, Inc., CORBIS; p.43, 87, 124, 126 © Norbert Schaefer/CORBIS; p.59, 64, 90–91, 108 © Ariel Skelley/CORBIS; p.71 © Cameron/CORBIS; p.79, 117 © Michael Keller/CORBIS; p.100–101 © Paul Barton/CORBIS; p.106 © Ted Horowitz/CORBIS; p.114 © Angela Wood/CORBIS; p.120 © Michael Prince/CORBIS; pp.112, 129 © Jutta Klee/CORBIS; p.130 © Jon Feingersh/CORBIS; p.143 © Bill Binzen/CORBIS; pp.150–151 © Jim Erickson/CORBIS; p.133 © Roy McMahon/CORBIS.

## Dedication

To my sister, Cathy, who shows us the meaning of generosity.

## Published by MQ Publications Limited

12 The Ivories
6–8 Northampton Street
London N1 2HY
Tel: +44 (0)20 7359 2244
Fax: +44 (0)20 7359 1616
Email: mail@mqpublications.com
Website: www.mqpublications.com

Editor: Karen Ball
Design concept: Balley Design Associates
Designer: Rod Teasdale
Photographer: Mike Prior

ISBN: 0-681-27880-3

1 3 5 7 9 0 8 6 4 2

Printed in China

# contents

# foreword

We are all familiar with stress—it's a fact of life. Modern life is lived at such a rapid pace that, increasingly, many of us find it difficult to keep up. Sadly the negative effects of the stress this causes are widespread and growing.

The body's stress response is triggered when we are faced with overwhelming demands. Whether these demands are large or small is of little consequence: it's the importance we attach to them that determines their impact. Important pressures that we don't feel we can cope with result in stress reactions and prolonged exposure to these reactions can have an impact on physical, emotional, and mental health.

Recent figures show that around two-thirds of us feel "stressed-out" at least once a month, and the majority of visits to doctors, and days off work, are triggered by stress-related problems. However, stress can also grow slowly and go unnoticed, or ignored, for years. Stress thrives when we lack time, information, and motivation, and can build up until something snaps under the pressure.

With this in mind, one of the most important life skills we can learn is the right way to manage stress. Once stress-busting skills are in place, you will find your mood becomes more stable, your thinking clears, and your relationships are strengthened. Just as importantly, your risk of suffering stress-related illness reduces.

This book aims to guide you through every aspect of stress management, providing you with a wide range of practical techniques to enhance your ability to recognize stress and effectively reduce it. Bear in mind that the most vital step you can make is to take action yourself. Don't just read this book; put its skills and strategies into action.

Otherwise, who knows, having it sitting on the bookshelf could even become a source of stress in itself! You begin to take action by making a commitment to yourself to put aside the time and effort needed to learn the new methods set out here. Do this and, by the end of the book, I guarantee you will have developed at least one strategy to turn to when you feel your stress levels rising.

The book opens with an explanation of exactly what stress is, then takes a look at some of the major causes of stress, and offers an interactive checklist to help you understand your current stress burden. By exploring the causes and effects of stress, you acquire a greater awareness of your current state of mind. Next come a series of practical step-by-step exercises to help you combat stress, many of which are flexible enough to build into your daily life. Lastly, there is useful and detailed advice on tackling the stress that builds up in response to specific life events, such as getting married or having children, changing job or moving home.

Relaxation and peace of mind are not reserved for those with pots of money and masses of free time; they can be yours, too, with a little knowledge and understanding. I hope the simple exercises and advice in this book will lighten your load and help you relax. For, above all, these stress-management tools aim to put you back where you belong—in control of your life!

**please note**

If you are pregnant, breast-feeding, or taking prescribed medication for any condition, only take herbal remedies and nutritional supplements following professional advice. If these restrictions do not apply, take the dose suggested on the bottle.

# chapter 1

# introduction

# what is stress?

## defining stress

To be able to recognize stress as it arises, it helps to understand what it is and how it occurs. One often-used definition characterizes stress as "the adverse reactions people have to excessive pressure or other types of demand placed on them, when those pressures are felt to be significant and to exceed the person's perceived coping ability." In layperson's language, stress is the tension we feel when the pressure is on and we don't feel able to manage it well.

Pressures on us—stressors—trigger a series of highly-tuned responses in body and mind, from raised blood pressure to racing thoughts. These days, stressors are often psychological rather than physical threats. This makes the effects more persistent and difficult to handle: there is no easy physical way to dissolve them, such as fighting or running away.

## how stress affects the body

The human stress response developed to equip us to cope with physically dangerous situations, setting up biological changes to prepare the body for action.

When we encounter a stressor, the "sympathetic" part of the autonomic nervous system (A.N.S.) triggers the release of a cocktail of chemicals into the bloodstream. These chemicals include adrenaline that causes a rapid rise in blood pressure and heart rate to increase bloodflow to the brain and muscles. Extra blood cells are released from bone marrow, helping it clot more easily and enabling wounds to heal. Blood sugar levels rise, making more energy available to the arms and legs, and blood moves away from the digestive system and the skin, where it's not immediately needed. Other consequences include faster breathing, a suppressed immune system, reduction in production of saliva, a release of pain-reliving endorphins, dilated pupils, and an enhancement of the five senses. All these changes help explain why we go pale, feel the heart racing, get a dry mouth, and generally feel very "switched on" under acute stress.

The stress response evolved as a survival mechanism to speed up decision-making and prepare body and mind to make a quick response to danger—either by fighting or fleeing. This is known as the "fight or flight" mechanism. However, this life-saving process developed when the typical threat was a hungry lion! The types of stressors faced by modern humans are quite different, comprising a set of complex and mundane irritations that ranges from being stuck in traffic to working for an overly-critical boss. Unfortunately, our bodies react to modern stressors with the same prehistoric fight or flight responses, which leaves us feeling over-alert, even panicky, with no easy way to resolve the situation. Our instinctual response to the situation—fighting or fleeing—denied, we ignore and override the resulting tiredness and anger. The energy remains unreleased and we still feel wound up. If this state of unresolved reaction continues, it can lead to symptoms that are potentially damaging to physical and emotional health. Some health experts believe that up to 80 percent of illness could be stress-related.

## Stress signals to look out for:

- a rise in your heart rate

- butterflies in your stomach

- dry mouth

- dilated pupils

- enhanced senses

- feeling panicky

- feeling over-alert

- a rush of energy

left > **Cardiovascular exercise can help alleviate the symptoms of our frustrated "fight or flight" instincts.**

## understanding stress

The stress response is sometimes useful in the short term—we need a certain amount of tension in order to give our best performance during an interview or while competing in sports. Problems arise when the stress response is sustained over a considerably longer time period.

Stress is not caused directly by the outside world, but by our reactions to it. This is determined, in part, by our personalities. Each of us perceives demands and pressures individually, and responds to them in different ways. An event such as public speaking that might make one person feel stressed may simply offer a bit of a buzz to someone else.

The variance in different personalities' responses to stress fluctuates according to how we perceive the demands, how much control we feel we have over them, and how much support we are given. Perfectionists who always want to do everything well are likely to feel stress more acutely. People who are more accepting of their limits tend to feel the effects less.

Another vital difference between people's stress-management skills is the importance they place on switching off. For example, many pressurized office workers don't take a break because they feel they don't have the time, or they think that taking time out might look unprofessional.

So, pressure in itself is not necessarily a bad thing, and many people thrive on it. It is when pressure is experienced as excessive that stress can develop into distress and sometimes disease.

Although we all differ in our susceptibility to stress, no matter how vulnerable we are to it, we can equip ourselves with techniques to help us cope.

"Once I realized no-one is perfect, it helped me relax instead of needing to be the best at everything I did."

**Mary, office manager**

## stress management

Stress management is a way of managing the pressures you face and reducing their negative impact on your wellbeing. Firstly, you need to work out the causes of your current stress in detail (see page 22). This helps you feel more in control. Then you can try a variety of practical techniques to help you manage life's pressures, from exercise, dietary changes, and time-management strategies to relaxation methods including meditation and aromatherapy. Through these and other tools you arrive at a stress action plan that fits your individual life, minimizing and treating the physical and emotional effects of stress as they affect you.

It's also important to look at the way you currently respond to stress. When you're

above > **A regular exercise program, such as yoga, is essential to managing stress.**

tearing your hair out, perhaps you go for a walk, have a relaxing bath, or pour it all out to a friend. These are good strategies. Others are less beneficial. "When it all gets too much in the office, I head straight outside for a cigarette break," admits Sue, a market researcher. Smoking, binge drinking, or comfort eating to ease stress only lead to further problems.

The strategies in this book will help you face up to your stressors and will give you the skills to deal with them successfully without jeopardizing your health.

# the long-term effects

## the role of the nervous system

**Long-term stress can have a serious impact on physical and psychological health because of the sustained high levels of chemicals released by the "fight or flight" response.**

The autonomic nervous system (A.N.S.) is a vast network of nerves reaching out from the spinal cord that affects every organ in the body. It has two branches—the sympathetic and the parasympathetic systems—that have opposite effects to each other. The sympathetic A.N.S. helps us deal with stressful situations by initiating the "fight or flight" response. Once the danger has passed, the parasympathetic A.N.S. takes over, decreasing the heartbeat and relaxing blood vessels.

In healthy people, the two branches of the autonomic nervous system maintain a balance– action followed by relaxation. Unfortunately, for many people, the sympathetic A.N.S. remains on guard, leaving them unable to relax and allow the parasympathetic system to take over.

## stress-related illness

If this situation is sustained over a period of time, a variety of stress-related symptoms and illnesses can ensue, and the problem is widespread. In the United Kingdom, an I.C.M. poll revealed that more than two-thirds of people believe they suffer from work-related stress, often with physical symptoms.

Some problems, such as headaches and muscle tension, are often directly caused by the body's responses that accompany stress. Many other disorders are aggravated by stress. Mind and body are inextricably linked, and the interaction between them produces physical changes: the brain notices a stressor, triggering a physical reaction that leads to further emotions and then mental and physical damage.

## don't despair

Before you read the long list of problems stress can cause on pages 16–21, bear in mind that you are not doomed! The human body is designed to withstand occasional extreme stress and can survive a good deal of pressure. Most of the problems outlined aren't life-threatening, and controling your stress levels will help keep them at bay. It's reassuring to remember that most damaging medical symptoms can be corrected if you take action in time. There is a great deal of expert help available out there, and if you are at all worried, don't delay in seeking it—peace of mind makes the effort worthwhile. The problem probably won't just go away, and the worst thing you can do is ignore it.

People vary in how much stress they can absorb before they snap. Only you know when you are reaching breaking point. If you do develop a stress-related disorder, see it as a chance to become familiar with your individual "weak point," and welcome the opportunity the illness brings for you to keep a close eye on it. If similar symptoms creep back again, heed them as a very serious warning, taking a close look at your current life and easing off the pressure wherever possible.

right > **Illustration of the nervous system—the network of nerves that branch off the spinal cord and carry messages as nerve impulses between the brain and the rest of the body.**

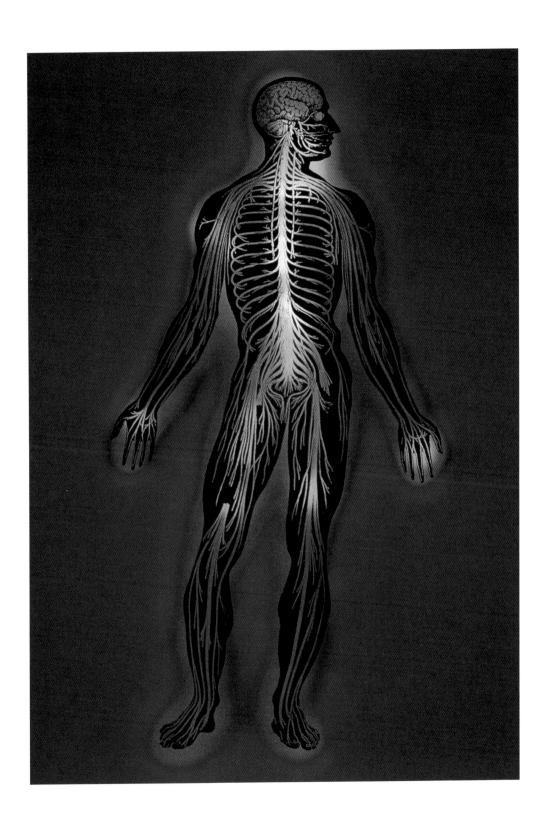

## stress-related health conditions

### heart disease

Over the long term, people who react more acutely to stress have a higher risk of cardiovascular disease—disorders of the heart and blood vessels, including heart attacks and strokes. This risk is particularly linked to people with a certain group of characteristics, known as a Type A personality. Such people tend to be excessively competitive, impatient, hostile, and move and talk quickly. Of these characteristics, hostility is often pinpointed as being the most significant.

The common stress response of eating comfort foods that are often full of fat and salt, is obviously not beneficial to the heart.

### high blood pressure

Know as hypertension, this is a very common chronic disease that usually shows no symptoms. Stress increases blood pressure in the short term. Chronic stress may contribute to a permanently raised blood pressure that increases the risk of suffering stroke, heart and kidney failure, and heart attack. If you have a family history of high blood pressure and heart

right > **People who suffer from high blood pressure would benefit from a relaxing exercise routine, such as simple yoga.**

problems, have regular checkups with your doctor, and try to follow his or her advice.

Other lifestyle habits may lead to hypertension. They include a diet high in saturated fat, a lack of physical activity, and consuming too much alcohol.

## susceptibility to infection

There is no doubt that when it is under stress, the immune system becomes suppressed, leaving the body more vulnerable to infection. Allergies and autoimmune diseases (including arthritis and multiple sclerosis) can be exacerbated by stress. This effect can be partly offset by social support from friends and family.

Being stressed also slows the rate at which you recover from illness.

## skin problems

Stress is known to aggravate skin problems such as acne, psoriasis, and eczema. It has also been linked to unexplained itchy skin rashes. These skin problems are in themselves intensely stressful.

## pain

Prolonged stress that stimulates the muscles continually can lead to muscular pain, such as backache. A sedentary lifestyle and bad posture only exacerbate the problem, helping make back, shoulder, and neckache an extremely widespread health complaint.

Stress is also thought to aggravate underlying painful conditions, such as herniated discs, fibromyalgia, and repetitive strain injury (R.S.I.). Most migraine sufferers will testify that stress contributes to headaches that can last for days.

## diabetes

There is some evidence that chronic stress can lead to insulin-dependent diabetes in people who are predisposed to the disease. This is because stress causes the immune system to destroy insulin-producing cells.

## infertility

Stress does not cause infertility, but the two have been linked many times. Couples who are trying for a baby are more likely to conceive on vacation or during periods of little stress, and fertility treatment given at these times is more successful, too. Welcome vacations not just for the reduction in stress hormones they bring, but for opportunities to conceive!

"When I'm under a lot of stress, I get a sharp pain in my lower back that can keep me off work for days."

**Tom, I.T. specialist**

# physical symptoms

Getting to know your physical responses to stress is the first step to take in stress-busting. Recognize them and you'll know when to start adopting stress-reduction tactics. Some of these symptoms affect everyone; others are more individual. But all are completely normal responses to being under pressure. There are short-term solutions to some of these symptoms, such as having a glass of water ready when public speaking, carrying headache or allergy meds, and not overeating before a situation you predict will be stressful. But if the symptoms continue for a sustained period of time, heed the message they are giving you.

## common physical symptoms of stress

- Pounding heart or palpitations: caused by an increased heart rate.

- Shivering and becoming pale: because blood has moved away from the skin.

- Sweating: helps the body keep cool in preparation for exertion.

- Headaches, dizziness, and faintness: from increased blood flow to the brain.

- Rapid breathing: to provide a flow of oxygen to the muscles.

- Insomnia: from a body and brain too "switched on" to sleep.

- Fatigue: caused by sustained arousal.

- Neck, shoulder, and backache/numbness: a result of prolonged muscular tension.

- Dry mouth or lump in the throat: occurs when less saliva is produced.

- Heightening of allergies or existing medical conditions: due to stress hormones.

- Feeling jumpy or shaky: from the buildup of stress hormones.

- Diarrhea or increased urination: prepares the body for faster escape.

- Bloating, nausea, indigestion, and butterflies in the stomach: results of a fluctuating blood supply to the digestive system.

- Increase in colds and infections: caused by suppression of the immune system.

- Increase in skin problems: may be exacerbated by stress hormones.

"I know it's all getting too much when I have several mouth ulcers at once."

**Anne, a banker**

## key stress-related disorders

### digestive problems

Because blood is diverted to the muscles as a result of the stress response, prolonged stress can disrupt the digestive system, leading to indigestion, diarrhea, constipation, cramping, bloating, or heartburn. In some people this progresses into I.B.S.—irritable bowel syndrome. This very common disorder, consisting of alternating constipation and diarrhea, is very poorly understood. Many possible causes have been suggested, but stress undoubtedly plays a part. Modern ways of eating, such as snacking on the run, only exacerbate digestive problems.

The stress-busting strategies in Chapter 2 (see page 38) may help ease symptoms.

### insomnia

The tension caused by unresolved stress can lead to sleep problems. Someone who is "stressed out" can find it difficult to sleep at nighttime, and may feel tired and lacking in energy during the day. This sleep deprivation sets up a negative spiral: most people who don't sleep are not in good shape to deal with the stresses of the following day.

It's a good idea to avoid caffeine and alcohol, and try out the stress-relieving solutions in Chapter 2 (see page 38).

### palpitations

Palpitations, an increased awareness of the heartbeat, are a quite normal reaction to stress, anxiety, or fear. Arrhythmias are disordered heartbeats—you might notice a missed beat, or a few grouped closely together. This can be very worrying. "I notice my heartbeat at nighttime and feel scared I'll have a heart attack," reports Katy, a journalist.

There is usually nothing to worry about. Reduce your alcohol and caffeine intake and adopt some of the stress-tackling techniques in Chapter 2 (see page 38). Consult your doctor if symptoms persist or if you experience any pain.

right > **Many people turn to alcohol as a short-term reliever of stress, but it can often exacerbate problems, acting as a depressant.**

# mental symptoms

Some of the most common mental and behavioral symptoms of stress are set out below. We have all experienced at least one of them at some point, but if you regularly experience any of these symptoms, you may need to visit your doctor for help or at least force yourself to take a break. Chapter 2 (see page 38) aims to equip you with the practical techniques and skills to reduce these unpleasant symptoms, or avoid them completely.

## common mental symptoms of stress

- Irritability

- Anxiety, fear, and worrying

- Depression, feelings of despair, and tearfulness

- Anger, frustration, and impatience

- Feeling insecure or paranoid

- Relying more on "props," such as cigarettes and alcohol

- Avoiding going to work, school, or university

- Avoiding friends and relatives

- More arguments with partner or family that may even lead to throwing objects or hitting out

- Insomnia and fatigue

- Increased clumsiness, fidgeting, or confusion

- Nail-biting

- Inability to make decisions or concentrate

- Memory problems

- Lack of care over diet and reliance on junk foods

- Over- or under-eating, or obsession with food

- Intrusive thoughts

- Obsessive-compulsive disorder

- Inability to switch off; mind racing or going blank

- Lack of enjoyment or sense of humor

- Self-harming

- Decreased libido

# key stress-related disorders

## depression

This is a very common response to chronic stress, even in animals. Some sadness is natural after upsetting events, but severe depression is far more than this, even if triggered by a major event, such as bereavement. Depression is a serious illness, bringing with it an increased risk of suicide. It changes how you think and affects your perceptions. It may seem like it will last forever, but there are many types of effective treatment available, including a variety of nonaddictive antidepressant drugs.

For more specific ways to understand and tackle depression, see Chapter 3 (page 100).

## anxiety

Most of us feel anxious when faced with great stress. In some people, this develops into an ongoing anxiety disorder that might include panic attacks. Anxiety disorders range from a generalized anxiety that has no obvious triggers to obsessive-compulsive disorder and post-traumatic stress disorder. Anxiety can cause a variety of physical symptoms including palpitations, sweating, and dizziness. On top of this, sufferers become even more sensitive to everyday stress. Sam, a dental nurse, says "My mind races and I can't make any sense of the confusion. I find myself constantly checking I've locked the front door and turned the oven off."

It is often a warning signal, not to be ignored. For specific ways to understand and tackle anxiety, see Chapter 3 (page 100).

## alcohol-related problems

Alcohol is frequently used to "drown our sorrows" or help us switch off after a long day. But excessive drinking can lead to alcoholism when it becomes a preoccupation and the drinking continues despite repeated alcohol-related problems. Heavy drinking increases the risk of mouth, throat, and other cancers (particularly in smokers), liver and heart disease, brain damage, stroke, and osteoporosis as well as social problems, such as losing a job or getting into trouble with the law. Symptoms of alcoholism include cravings, impaired control, physical dependence, and increased tolerance.

Alcohol can be as hard to give up as illegal drugs; you may need professional help to cut down (see page 154).

## nicotine-related problems

Smoking is closely linked to stress. Many smokers either feel that it helps them calm down or perks them up. The reality is that nicotine is a stimulant, and so is unlikely to be calming, at least physically. The important destressing factor might be the break taken to smoke the cigarette and the deep breathing involved in the action rather than the nicotine itself. Smoking is linked to countless diseases, a large proportion of which are fatal, so it is essential that you try to stop at once.

There is a great deal of help available for those who choose to quit smoking (consult your doctor or health visitor). But the biggest step is deciding that you truly want to quit.

# how stressed are you?

On the next few pages you will find a stress-scale exercise that helps you work out how much stress you are currently facing. Your score gives a rough indication of how susceptible you are at present to mental and physical illness, and acts as a "warning light," if you are at risk, that you should reduce the stress in your life.

The scale is based on the idea that the effects of major events accumulate as the number of events mount up. So the more events (both good and bad) you are exposed to, the greater your level of stress. A value is assigned to key life events you might have experienced over the last 12 months. Feel free to add others you think might be relevant, giving them a score based on those most similar in the scale.

Of course, the impact major life events have on mind and body varies enormously between individuals because of factors as diverse as personality and financial status. Still, this exercise provides a good starting point for assessing your life as it is now.

## the stress scale

Add up the values of each event you have experienced in the past year to arrive at your total score. You will find an assessment of your results on pages 24 to 25.

| event | score | event | score |
|---|---|---|---|
| 1 Death of a spouse | 100 | 15 Business readjustments | 39 |
| 2 Divorce | 73 | 16 Change in financial state | 38 |
| 3 Marital separation | 65 | 17 Death of a close friend | 37 |
| 4 Jail term | 63 | 18 Change to different line of work | 36 |
| 5 Death of a close family member | 63 | 19 Change in number of arguments | |
| 6 Personal injury or illness | 53 | with spouse | 35 |
| 7 Marriage | 50 | 20 Mortgage over one year's salary | 31 |
| 8 Fired at work | 47 | 21 House repossessed | 30 |
| 9 Marital reconciliation | 45 | 22 Change in responsibilities at work | 29 |
| 10 Retirement | 45 | 23 Son or daughter leaving home | 29 |
| 11 Change in health of family member | 44 | 24 Trouble with in-laws | 29 |
| 12 Pregnancy | 40 | 25 Outstanding personal | |
| 13 Sexual difficulties | 39 | achievements | 28 |
| 14 Gain of a new family member | 39 | 26 Spouse begins or stops work | 26 |

"Giving birth for the first time was an amazing experience. But taking that baby home and learning how to cope was a whole different ball game."

Alex, rights manager

| event | score | event | score |
|---|---|---|---|
| 27 Begin or end school or university | 26 | 36 Change in social activities | 18 |
| 28 Change in living conditions | 25 | 37 Loan less than one year's salary | 17 |
| 29 Revision of personal habits | 24 | 38 Change in sleeping habits | 16 |
| 30 Trouble with boss | 23 | 39 Change in number of | |
| 31 Change in work hours or conditions | 20 | family get-togethers | 15 |
| 32 Change in residence | 20 | 40 Change in eating habits | 15 |
| 33 Change in school or university | 20 | 41 Vacation | 13 |
| 34 Change in recreational activities | 19 | 42 Christmas or other major holiday | 12 |
| 35 Change in religious activities | 19 | 43 Minor violations of law | 11 |

## your results

Once you have arrived at your total score, find the category below that it fits within to read about your current susceptibility to illness and other stress-related problems.

### Below 150—low level of stress

You have a 30 percent probability of developing an illness within the next year. This is the average chance everyone has of getting ill, so don't let it worry you. Keep using the stress-relieving strategies you currently employ.

### Between 150 and 22—mild level of stress

You have a 40 percent probability of becoming ill. Although there are transitions taking place in your life, you may not feel you need to take any action yet. However, it is important that you learn how to cope more effectively with stress (see page 38), and steer clear of avoidable stressful situations.

### Between 225 and 300—moderate level of stress

You have a 60 percent probability of developing an illness. You may be having trouble concentrating for any length of time, be suffering from insomnia, and feeling generally irritated and emotional. Everyday chores are probably a struggle. This is a sign that you need to improve your stress-management skills (see page 38).

### Over 300—serious level of stress

If your score is over 300, your probability of becoming ill jumps to 80 percent. This is dangerous, and your risk of developing heart problems is high. You are probably going through a time of major transition and can only take so much before something snaps. Stress management should now be a top priority, so turn immediately to page 38.

## making sense of your results

This exercise should have helped to clarify your personal stress situation. Maybe just completing the exercise has shed light on circumstances, allowing you to understand a little more about why you are feeling stressed. The scale highlights the relative importance of family events over work problems in relation to stress. This is worth bearing in mind—often people believe the workplace to be their biggest stressor. The scale does not cover pressures indirectly related to your daily life, such as the political, environmental, or economic climate. Of course, these affairs do affect us, and must be regarded as an additional source of stress. Also not covered by the scale, but more directly related to everyday living, are the daily mini-stressors that are always with us, slowly accumulating to increase the tension. These are the focus of pages 26-27.

After completing the survey you may sense the stress as more urgent. If you feel you need outside help, do not delay in approaching a friend, relative, or doctor. You might also like to try the exercise again, this time predicting your score for the 12 months ahead. If the score is higher than you would ideally like it to be (a common pattern), think about ways of minimizing the impact of each event, and take reassurance from the unavoidable nature of some of the stress (remember, it's not your fault).

The type of illness stress may cause varies enormously between one individual and another. It might inflame your "weak spot"—perhaps you are prone to migraines or digestive problems—or take the form of something more serious. Keep a close eye on your own health and don't ignore unusual symptoms. No one knows your body and its health as well as you do.

"I hadn't even noticed that I was taking my moods out on my partner. Once I managed to sort out my insomnia problems, the first thing I did was apologize to my husband!"

**Clare, human resources manager**

# everyday stressors

## identifying regular stressors

The gradual accumulation of everyday hassles might be more significant to your wellbeing than one-off life events. Focusing on these smaller but more numerous stress factors could give the most accurate picture of your current stress level.

Anything can set off the body's stress response. Common aspects of life that produce ongoing stress include the following:

- **Financial issues**

- **Workplace problems**

- **Marital difficulties**

- **Family conflicts**

- **Commuting**

- **Health—yours and that of those close to you**

- **Overcrowding**

- **Time pressure**

- **Routine and boredom**

- **Unpredictable events**

The more of these hassles you experience, the greater your risk of developing negative symptoms. Such chronic stressors keep the pressure on by sustaining the body's "fight or flight" response, a physiological mechanism only designed to last a few minutes. When stress chemicals are continuously released, the heart rate remains high and the immune system is suppressed, and so little niggles sustain ongoing health problems, including anxiety and depression. Rats kept in this state eventually die of exhaustion!

In some people constant stress produces a feeling of helplessness, but most of us keep pushing ourselves onward. Most important is to focus this energy in the most beneficial way. Most of these small stressors can't be avoided, but some can be reduced. Spend a few minutes each day thinking about creative ways to ease the demands put on you. Feeling you can do something about the situation will help you feel more in control—an important part of your stress management.

## keeping a stress diary

Sometimes it's hard to identify why we feel so stressed. Keeping a stress diary is useful because it helps locate the cause of feelings by pinpointing the moment at which they begin. It also helps by revealing patterns in behavior and stress responses that can lead to a positive change.

**Here is one way to use a stress diary; adapt the ideas to suit your own lifestyle.**

1 Write the days of the week at the top of a page in a notebook, or your regular diary if there is sufficient space. Divide the day into sections—by hours, into quarters or thirds, or for a.m, p.m, evening, and night.

above > **Keeping a stress diary is a small but significant step toward understanding and conquering patterns of stress.**

2 As soon as possible after feeling a stress symptom, note it down, with a record of the events leading up to it. Write down everything you feel is relevant, including your thoughts before, during, and after the event. Also record your reactions and be honest, even if you regret them!

3 Aim to update the diary several times a day for a week. Continue for as long as is needed for you to start identifying your triggers and responses.

4 Look to your diary for insight. You might resist reaching certain conclusions because they're not what you want to believe. The insight a diary brings can be challenging, even painful, and point toward changes you don't want to make.

5 Take as much or as little action as you are ready for. What's most important is to begin to understand your stress responses.

# coping strategies

Although personality governs the way in which we respond to stressful situations, altering their impact for good or bad, each of us can learn to use more productive coping strategies. Making strong choices takes courage to start with. But with each use, new and positive habits become more instinctive, and unhealthy choices become less and less attractive. There is no need to live a dull life of self-denial and rigid discipline. Nor should you let a fear of monotony put you off taking action against stress. Stress management is about getting all you can from life.

## negative strategies

We have all fallen back on unhealthy coping strategies at one time or another. Whether it's drinking heavily, biting fingernails, or pushing ourselves too hard, we all have bad habits. Often these bad habits only create more stress—ever put off work till the last minute then run out of time to complete it? Attempt to transform each bad habit into a good habit. This isn't easy. Pick just one unhelpful response to stress and work away at it over a week or more until it's gone for good. Be patient and don't give up. Try also replacing bad habits with some of the wide range of alternative responses to stress set out opposite. None of these will make the original problems worse. For more practical details on these individual strategies, turn to Chapter 2 (see page 38).

## positive strategies

• Take exercise: a great way to release frustrations and clear the mind. You'll feel healthier too.

• Begin yoga: particularly appropriate for dealing with stress.

• Practice relaxation, deep breathing, and meditation: all counteract the effects of stress on mind and body.

- Book a massage or some aromatherapy: to get you back in touch with your body.

- Spend time in nature: it brings all your senses together.

- Resurrect hobbies and become more creative: often neglected when the pressure is on, these activities help you enjoy your life again.

- Play some tunes: closely tied to emotions, music can calm or bring on a burst of energy.

- Laugh a little: it may seem unimportant under stress, but humor offers a great way to release tension.

- Feed yourself good food: nutrition is important for everyone, but especially when stress is draining your resources.

- Sleep well: sleep provides a much-needed break, and gives you more energy.

- Gain self-awareness and perspective: knowing your patterns and habitual responses helps you work with, not against, your true nature.

- Use constructive self-talk: boosts your confidence, and with greater confidence it's easier to confront problems.

- Plan ahead: setting goals and priorities helps you get where you want to be.

- Manage your time effectively: reduce the sense of chaos and simplify your life.

- Seek support: friends, workmates, and family can be essential—some events cannot be dealt with on your own.

- Use counseling and other professional support: this might be necessary in certain situations. The help you need is out there awaiting your call.

## quick ways to cope with overwhelming stress

- **Take a break to remove yourself from the situation.**

- **Breathe deeply and slowly for a few minutes.**

- **Have a relaxing bath or go for a walk.**

- **Ask for help—delegate or share responsibility.**

- **Write down your thoughts so they begin to make sense.**

- **Do just one thing at a time.**

- **Reduce your standards, if only temporarily.**

- **Meet up with supportive friends and let off steam.**

- **Book a day off work or a vacation as soon as possible.**

## assessing your current coping strategies

Because the danger of stress derives from the way in which we respond to stressors, it is important to understand those habitual responses. In the spaces below, write down your regular responses to feeling stressed. For example, taking time out for a break, breathing deeply, or snapping at a workmate. Be honest, even if it sounds unpleasant. Next, evaluate each of your habitual responses, considering whether it works or not, both in the short and long term. Consider also whether you are happy or unhappy about your response, and whether you'd like to keep using it or abandon it.

### how I respond to stress right now

| regular response | evaluation |
| --- | --- |
| I yell at colleagues. | Makes them aggressive and defensive and I feel guilty. Not good for morale at work. |
| | |
| | |
| | |
| | |
| | |

## new strategies

Now record the new strategies you'd like to try out, perhaps taking inspiration from the ideas set out on page 29. Note down the benefits you expect to gain from each strategy, and spell out how you plan to incorporate it into your daily or weekly life. For example, you might plan to meditate for 10 minutes first thing in the morning, rent a funny D.V.D. tonight, or go swimming every Saturday afternoon.

## how I'd like to respond to stress

| new strategy | benefits | action to take |
|---|---|---|
| Get to lunchtime yoga class. | I'm more chilled in the afternoon when the shop is extra busy. | Arrange lunchtime cover. |
| | | |
| | | |
| | | |
| | | |
| | | |

# what can you change?

Of course, one of the most useful ways of managing stress is actually to eliminate unnecessary sources of stress. Here, we help you work out what stressors you have control over, and therefore can change, and which are unavoidable. You can change your routine to avoid being rushed before work, for example, but may not have total control over your housing, finance, or health. In fact, we only really have control over our own actions. Trying to exert control over anything else could be fighting a losing battle.

What we do have full control over is our response to stress and the decisions we make. Realizing this can help us to adapt to problems and find solutions to them. A sense of control can dramatically reduce feelings of stress. One way to achieve this is to predict sources of stress before they arise, then do what we can to avoid them, or prepare to lessen their impact.

## assessing what you can change

Look back over your stress diary (see page 26) and list five things you have the power to alter, and any thoughts on how you might do so. For example, you can control the amount of time you have before work by setting your alarm clock for earlier, and reduce your panic by getting your work clothes ready the night before. Or you could plan to go to the supermarket at a quieter time to avoid waiting so long at the checkout.

### things I can change

| 1 | |
|---|---|
| 2 | |
| 3 | |
| 4 | |
| 5 | |

## accepting what you can't change

Now comes the hard part. Not giving up because we can't change something, but finding the strength to accept reality. It takes a great deal of courage to accept our lack of control over aspects of life. Unexpected and unpleasant events are inevitable; we don't have complete control over other people and situations, and life never was meant to be easy! What we can do is avoid unnecessary stress by not trying to change other people and circumstances outside our remit. Fighting against the grain only leads to anger and frustration, and wastes energy. Trying to control ourselves too much also increases stress. Rather than setting very high standards, such as never being late or making mistakes, try to accept yourself as you are—no one is perfect.

Now list five things you can't change, and ways you can think of to reevaluate and come to terms with them. For example, maybe you can't avoid waiting in the bus queue, but you could use your time there to plan your goals for the day.

| things I can't change | | how to get over it |
|---|---|---|
| 1 | | |
| 2 | | |
| 3 | | |
| 4 | | |
| 5 | | |

# are you ready to manage stress?

The world around us is constantly altering and progressing. To be truly relaxed and go with the flow we must be prepared to change. This requires an open mind and belief in our own strength. To develop new techniques for managing stress, you need to stay flexible and be willing to try new things. This might feel like the last thing you need, but is necessary if your current responses to stress aren't working successfully. Your present actions and attitudes may be keeping you stuck in a cycle of stress. Change does not need to be difficult or scary—the last thing you need is another source of pressure! Take change at your own pace, but try to remain open to new ideas, and get over the common get-out excuses that block change and are set out on the opposite page.

right > **An open mind and self belief are crucial to managing stress, and meditation is a practical way of calming the inner spirit and finding peace of mind.**

# common get-outs

## lack of time
You may believe you just don't have time to include another activity in your life. But many stress-management strategies take no time at all, and might even help you feel more in control of your time.

## fear
Are you scared of entering into the unknown? If you have always approached life with the same beliefs, altering them may seem not just scary, but even impossible. For example, the thought of lowering self-imposed standards might bring up a fear of not being "good enough." Investigate your dread of changing and evaluate how realistic it is. You may find your apprehensions are based on past experience and no longer apply or stand up to reason. As you work through your fears, and your change of behavior does not cause catastrophes, you will develop more confidence in the process and in yourself.

## lack of motivation
Try to imagine an improved life for yourself and for your family and friends. By now you should begin to see just how much you could gain by being on top of your stress levels. Remind yourself afresh of all these benefits when all the effort to destress just seems to be far too much hassle.

## procrastination
Perhaps you have the motivation, but tend to procrastinate. "I'll start tomorrow/next week/ on January 1..." is the common cry. Sadly this magical day often never comes. Procrastination is often a complicated problem involving issues such as guilt, inadequacy, and depression. Try to discern the underlying cause and you could uncover some important issues that need to be worked through.

## scepticism
Some people remain sceptical about the concept of stress even though many readers and research studies find that it is a very real issue that must be addressed if one is to avoid chronic health problems. Of course it is sensible to be sceptical about "miracle cures," and other schemes designed to part you from your money. But the stress-management techniques explored in this book are based on common sense and good science. Suspend your disbelief and give them a try.

# summary

- Many situations can trigger a physical response to stress.

- If sustained, this response may be damaging to your physical and emotional health.

- Stress is caused by your reaction to a situation, not the situation itself.

- It is important to understand your individual response to stress so you can recognize it as it arises.

- You can equip yourself with techniques to help you cope.

- Coping strategies can be positive or negative.

- Stress management is the ability to manage pressure and lessen its impact on your wellbeing.

- Learning new responses takes effort, commitment, and an open mind.

# notes

# stress-busting strategies

get active

relax mind and body

get a massage

self-massage

enjoy nature

be creative

become self-aware

gain perspective

use positive self-talk

build on your strengths

- set goals
- establish priorities
- manage your time
- be confident
- communicate effectively
- build social support
- seek counseling
- eat well
- get quality sleep
- summary

# get active

Nothing beats regular exercise as a way of reducing stress. When stressed, the body goes into a state of high arousal, as a result of the "fight or flight" reaction. Usually, there is nowhere for that energy to go, so the body remains in this agitated state for hours at a time. Exercise is the best way to dissipate excess energy, especially if you have a sedentary job. Channel it into proper exercise rather than pacing up and down or drumming your fingers!

## getting over excuses

If you find yourself making excuses, write them down and assess each one in the cold light of day. Here are the most common:

• I don't have the time: build exercise into your life by taking the stairs instead of the elevator or getting off the bus one stop early.

• It's too expensive: exercise isn't limited to leisure centers and gyms—go for a jog or a brisk walk, which come for free.

• I am not the athletic type/I'm no good at sport: exercise doesn't require a particular skill—gardening, and vigorous vacuuming count too.

• I don't enjoy exercise: take dancing classes or try cycling to work.

• I am too old/tired/overweight/self-conscious: everyone feels less tired following exercise, and after a few weeks of regular sessions you'll notice the pounds dropping off.

• There are no facilities close by: workout at home by climbing stairs, following a yoga video, or playing ball with the kids.

• I can't be bothered: have a look at the motivation tips opposite.

Exercise doesn't have to be limited to playing sport at a leisure center or pacing the gym treadmill. Read on for tips on alternative ways to exercise.

## motivation tips

Experts recommend a minimum of 30 minutes' exercise at a moderate intensity most days of the week. When you can't raise the motivation, pause to consider the benefits of exercising.

- **Lowers risk of illness: physical activity reduces the likelihood of several chronic diseases and health conditions, including diabetes, heart attack, and stroke.**

- **Eases existing health problems: exercise can help to manage high blood pressure and back pain, but check with your doctor before beginning a program.**

- **Promotes quality sleep: exercise not only improves your health and reduces stress, it relaxes tense muscles and helps you sleep.**

- **Gives a psychological boost: physical activity causes the release of chemicals called endorphins into the bloodstream, making you feel relaxed and happy. This can be a helpful tool in fighting depression and anxiety.**

- **Keeps the body in shape: physical activity tones muscles and helps you to shed the pounds.**

- **Boosts stress management: as well as having an outlet for the excess energy produced by stress in the short term, people who exercise regularly are more equipped to handle the long-term effects of stress.**

## ways to exercise

- Try a brisk walk, run, bike ride, or game of squash: you don't need to join a gym; taking exercise can be as informal as walking the dog or dancing at home to a favorite C.D.

- Sample swimming, jogging, cycling, aerobics classes or videos: all are great forms of exercise and when you discover an activity you enjoy, it won't feel like a chore.

left > **A brisk walk is not only invigorating and enjoyable—it can be the first step toward a new stress-reducing exercise routine.**

- Vary activities to avoid boredom: if you take your regular exercise in the gym, try an outdoor activity.

- Keep it fun: it's difficult to maintain motivation for a regime that you dislike. Exercise with a friend to encourage you to keep up the good work, and try activities that help you forget you're exercising, such as rollerblading or flying a kite.

- To avoid injury, always warm up before starting an activity: and cool down well afterward, making sure you stretch all the major muscle groups.

# which form of exercise?

**Particular types of exercise lend themselves well to stress-busting. Below are details of three of the most suitable forms, followed by suggestions for some simple exercises.**

## walking

Even the least fit can incorporate some walking into a daily routine. An organized walking regime offers a great form of aerobic exercise. It is free, and strengthens the heart and lungs as well as the legs. It also helps prevent osteoporosis, lowers blood pressure and cholesterol levels, helps with diabetes, and increases flexibility.

Aim for the easily achievable target of walking for 30 minutes most days. You might walk all or part of the way to work, or take one 15 minute burst at lunchtime and another in the evening. As your fitness improves, you could even try alternating walking with slow jogging. After a few weeks' practice, you'll find yourself instinctively walking up stairs instead of taking the elevator.

## yoga

Yoga reduces stress and improves strength, flexibility, coordination, circulation, and posture. It may even reduce the frequency of asthma attacks. The discipline is an ancient Indian practice, dating back more than 5000 years. The word *yoga* means union, and was originally designed to lead to union of the human spirit with nature. However, today many people use it as a technique to link the body and mind in a way that encourages peacefulness and relaxation.

Yoga employs stretching postures, breathing, and meditation techniques to calm the mind and tone the body. There are many different schools of practice, but almost all the forms taught in the West are types of Hatha Yoga, a combination of *asanas* (physical exercises and postures), *pranayama* (breath-control techniques), and meditation.

Although it is possible to learn about yoga from books and videos, the best way is to attend a class led by an experienced and enthusiastic instructor.

## t'ai chi

Also known as *t'ai chi ch'uan*, this ancient form of martial art helps to reduce stress and improve strength and flexibility. Based in the Chinese Taoist philosophy, it was developed in order to encourage health, self-defence, and spiritual development.

The practice combines a series of gentle physical movements with breathing techniques, allowing you to experience a meditative state. The idea is that it facilitates the flow of *chi* ("life energy") throughout the body by dissolving blockages within the body and between the body and the environment. Through concentration, coordinated breathing, and slow, graceful body movements, t'ai chi aims to increase wellbeing. It has recently been established that older people who practice t'ai chi are at reduced risk of falls, because of its beneficial effect on balance.

T'ai chi is now practiced all over the world. As with yoga, it's always best to learn from a qualified teacher.

right > **T'ai chi is an ancient exercise system that the modern world has embraced. Not only does it keep you strong and flexible, it also encourages your spiritual development.**

# Salute to the sun

Salute to the sun is a series of movements that flow into each other, coordinated by in and out breaths. It is a cornerstone of any yoga practice and good to learn. It not only exercises your limbs, joints, and muscles, but is a good meditative exercise that brings you to a state of calm.

1 Stand facing north with feet and hands together. Make sure your body is in correct alignment with your bottom tucked in, abdominals sucked in, and shoulders dropped. If it helps, imagine there is a thread pulling up from the crown of your head. Close your eyes and visualize the sun.

2 With an inhalation, extend your arms out by your sides, and then up overhead. Try to keep your shoulders relaxed. Look up at your fingertips, then stretch backward gently, being careful to go back only as far as is comfortable.

3 Exhaling, bend forward from the hips, and place your palms on either side of your feet, relaxing your head between your arms. Keep the back straight as you bend forward and down—don't collapse down into this position. When you first practice this you will probably need to bend your knees, unless you are already very flexible. With time, your legs will straighten.

4 On the next inhalation, take the left leg back as far as you can into a lunge position, right heel remaining flat on the floor and hips facing forward. Look up.

5 Take the right leg back and hold yourself in a push-up position, looking slightly forward. Concentrate on keeping the back flat rather than allowing your lower back and abdominals to collapse down toward the floor.

6 On an inhalation, allow your knees, hips, and chest to lower to the floor. Control the movement and lower yourself slowly.

7 With the next exhalation, push your hips toward the sky, extend out of the shoulders, and work to press the heels down.

8 Step your left leg forward with an inhalation back into the lunge pose and look up again, as in step 4.

9 Bring your right leg forward with an exhalation and push your tailbone to the sky, working to straighten the knees, as in step 3.

10 Draw your hands into prayer position overhead with an inhalation. Open your arms and extend backward, as in step 2.

11 Bring your hands back into prayer position in front of your chest with the exhalation, bowing your head. Repeat all the steps, this time working with the opposite leg.

# relax mind and body

When you feel anxious, relaxation techniques can help ease the tension from body and mind and divert your attention from the problems at hand. Try out as many of the techniques on pages 48–53 as you can to find which works best for you.

## progressive relaxation

Progressive, or muscular, relaxation produces a response that is the opposite of the "flight or flight" mechanism. It lowers blood pressure and reduces anxiety. By decreasing muscle tension, progressive relaxation helps diffuse the stiff muscles, clenched jaw, and frowns that can set in during a day spent working at a desk. Try to find time to follow these steps every day, avoiding periods when you are sleepy and immediately after a meal.

### how to do it

1 Put on loose clothing that allows you to move and breathe freely. Eliminate distractions and put on some calm music if it relaxes you.

2 Sit or lie comfortably and close your eyes. Let your breathing become deeper and slower. After a few moments, focus on relaxing the muscles in your toes. If it helps, tense the muscles for a few seconds, then relax them. Repeat this process as many times as you need until the toes are relaxed and heavy.

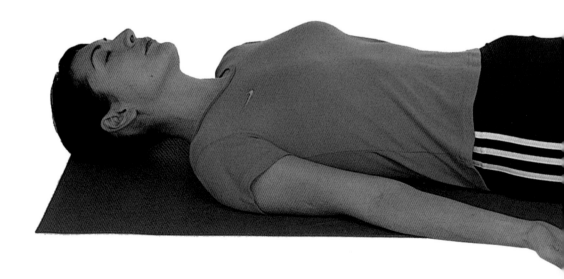

3 Concentrate on your foot, then your ankle, tensing and relaxing all the muscles as before. Lift your foot from the ground, if necessary, before allowing it to drop heavy and relaxed.

4 When the muscles feel truly relaxed, move up the leg and repeat as before. Continue in the same way up your torso, squeezing and releasing your buttocks, abdomen, and chest. Then work on the arms, neck, shoulders, and lastly your head.

5 Lie still for a few minutes feeling every part of your body heavy and completely relaxed.

6 Whenever you recognize that your muscles are tense, repeat the exercise. The more you practice, the easier it becomes.

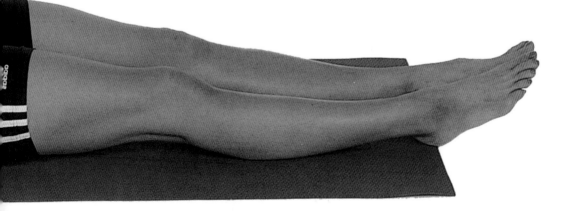

## deep breathing

Controlled breathing is a valuable stress-relieving tool that some people find is the key to calming body and mind. How we breathe reflects the way we are feeling—shallow and rapid when anxious, deep and slow when relaxed. Breathing lightly makes less oxygen available for the body, and does not fully expel carbon dioxide. This can lead to tiredness and dizziness. If you notice yourself breathing quickly and only from the upper chest, use this simple breathing exercise to relax your muscles and mind and increase energy levels.

### how to do it

1 Sit comfortably. Close your eyes if it helps you feel more relaxed.

2 Place one hand on your chest and the other low on your abdomen.

3 Make sure your mouth is closed. Breathe in slowly and deeply through the nose, trying to breathe so that the hand on your chest remains still. Feel the lower hand move as the abdomen expands with the inhalation.

above and below> **There are a number of different sitting positions you can use when practising deep breathing, from cross-legged to full lotus.**

4 Retain the breath for a few moments. Both hands should be motionless.

5 Breathe out slowly through the mouth, feeling your lower hand being drawn toward your lower back.

6 Repeat as many times as necessary until you feel calm.

## progressive relaxation

Meditation is a specific form of relaxation that can help alleviate stress and feelings of panic. Practiced regularly, it increases your sense of control and allows you to confront stressful situations more positively. In terms of good health, meditation can help reduce insomnia, high blood pressure, headaches, and asthma. It can aid performance at work and in exams, and encourage creativity. Regular meditation may even help prevent some of the effects of ageing, and lead to improved memory, vision, and hearing. For some people it might be enough to meditate infrequently, but most people derive optimum benefits from sessions once or twice daily, or at the minimum a couple of times a week. If you have trouble meditating at home, find a class to get expert tuition.

### how to do it

1 Find somewhere quiet away from distractions. Sit comfortably, either cross-legged on the floor or on a hard-backed chair with feet flat on the floor. Keep your spine straight, supporting your stance by placing cushions beneath your knees or buttocks, or using the support of a wall.

2 Rest your hands on your knees or thighs and close your eyes. Watch your regular breath moving in and out for a minute or so, then focus on making the breath longer, deeper, and more even.

3 Focus your attention on a mantra, a word or phrase of your choice that makes you feel calm, such as "breathe," "love," or "peace." Any word with personal meaning will do. Alternatively, concentrate on the even flow in and out of your breath, or steady your eyes on an object of focus, such as the flame of a candle or a crystal placed at eye level.

4 Over time, build up to 20 minutes' practice. It is inevitable that your mind will wander. Don't be annoyed. Calmly accept the thought and slowly regain your concentration.

# visualization

There are at least two ways of using visualization. Here are two methods that might prove useful in your battery of stress-relief tactics. The first allows you to play out stressful scenarios in your mind, developing alternative ways to react to similar events in the future. The second technique is a coping strategy that defuses stressful situations.

## how to do it at home

1 Choose a quiet time and place at home. Sit comfortably and close your eyes. Go back to a recent situation in which you became stressed, anxious, or angry.

2 Picture yourself back there, but reacting in a different way. Try to put the event into perspective and imagine yourself responding rationally. Then feel the satisfaction of knowing you stayed calm and managed the situation positively.

## how to do it in times of stress

1 When you are calm, take a few minutes to concentrate on the most relaxing experience you can remember—an afternoon on a quiet beach, or a long candlelit bath perhaps. Picture it in detail, focusing on each of your senses in turn.

2 When you feel stress levels rising, take a moment to recall the relaxing scene. Let this help you step back from what's happening and see its real significance. At first, shifting attention from the matter in hand might seem awkward and unnecessary. Once you have experienced the benefits it becomes easier.

below > **The memory of a relaxing bath can be a useful image to have during visualization.**

# get a massage

Many people use massage as a guaranteed path to relaxation. Touch is an effective and reliable stress-reliever because it leads to the release of endorphins, producing a feeling of wellbeing. Massage reduces stress hormones, alleviates anxiety, and eases tense muscles. There are numerous types, but most use a carrier (or base) oil, either unscented or mixed with essential oils (aromatherapy).

## types of massage

### back, neck, and shoulder massage
Effective because so much tension is stored here. Under stress, the body's posture tends to become worse, especially when submitted to the stress and neck strain that comes from hunching over a computer for hours. Tiredness can also lead to bad posture. Massage helps unravel the knots. See the following pages for details of how to self-massage.

### full body massage
As a luxurious treat, this is an extremely effective way of combating stress. The strokes can be gentle or quite intense for deep release of muscular tension.

### Indian head massage
Usually performed while you sit in a chair, this works on the shoulders, neck, head, and face. The aim is to improve bloodflow to the upper body, increasing oxygen and so the supply of nutrients to the muscles. Scalp massage is also said to promote hair growth, relieve eyestrain, headaches and insomnia, and lead to improved concentration.

### reflexology
The 72,000 nerve endings in the feet are connected to different organs of the body. By massaging, rotating, and applying pressure to zones on the foot, ankle, and toes, a reflexologist aims to encourage energy flow, in so doing reducing tension and correcting problems that can lead to ill health. Some therapists work on the hands or earlobes.

### shiatsu
This form of Japanese massage is based on a similar premise to acupuncture—exerting pressure along key points on meridians, or energy paths, around the body to affect the good functioning of organs. It also includes elements of osteopathy. The therapy is seen as more preventative than healing, and practitioners recommend it is undertaken as part of a healthy lifestyle. As with reflexology, the aim is to allow proper energy flow around the body. A shiatsu massage can be quite intense, the masseur using elbows, knees, and feet as well as hands to exert pressure.

### aromatherapy
Essential oils are often blended to use during massage for their ability to stimulate or relax mind and body, or for a specific healing purpose. They can also be inhaled by heating 3–4 drops in an oil vaporizer, adding 8–10 drops to a bath, or placing 2 drops on a handkerchief or pillow. Essential oils are extracted from the leaves, petals, roots, and bark of plants. Over 400 varieties exist, each believed to have unique therapeutic properties.

## stress-relieving essential oils

### lavender
Possibly the most useful stress-busting essential oil. Valued for its antidepressant and sedative properties, and to help reduce high blood pressure and intestinal disorders. Avoid during the first trimester of pregnancy and with low blood pressure.

### camomile
Used to relieve stomach disorders and headaches and to promote sleep. Valued for its soothing, anxiety-relieving action. Avoid during the first trimester of pregnancy.

### jasmine
Employed in the treatment of depression and postnatal depression, and enjoyed for its restorative and confidence-raising qualities. Avoid during pregnancy.

### rose
Another depression-lifting oil particularly recommended for women. Also used to treat stomach and heart disorders. Emotionally healing, it also boosts positivity. Avoid during pregnancy.

### ylang ylang
A relaxing oil valued for its ability to calm over-rapid breathing and heart rate, and lower raised blood pressure. Use in low doses to avoid headaches, nausea, and skin irritation.

### peppermint
Recommended for tension headaches and stress-related stomach problems. Valued for lifting fatigue and depression. Use in low doses and avoid if you are pregnant, breastfeeding, or have sensitive skin.

**please note**
Consult a qualified aromatherapist before using oils if pregnant or breastfeeding. After using most citrus oils avoid exposing skin to sunlight (even on cloudy days) as they may cause skin irritation. Always buy oils from a reputable retailer and refer to cautions on the bottle.

# self-massage for back, neck, and shoulders

Self-massage can be an effective, spontaneous reliever of stress. All you need is a moment to yourself and your own pair of hands!

## stroking

1 Gently tilt your head to the right and place one hand (fingers and thumbs together) on the back of the shoulder, supporting your arm at the elbow with your other hand.

2 Stroke down the side of the neck and back of the shoulder from your hairline. Lift the hand away and return it to your starting position to repeat the stroke.

## circular pressure

1 Maintaining the same arm position, make deep, slow, circular strokes with the fingertips all over the back of your opposite shoulder, wherever the muscles feel tense and tight.

2 Repeat the stroke over the side of the neck.

## squeeze and hold

Again in the same supported arm position, grasp the muscle on the top of the shoulder between the heel of your hand and your fingertips. Squeeze the muscle and hold for 8–10 seconds before gently releasing.

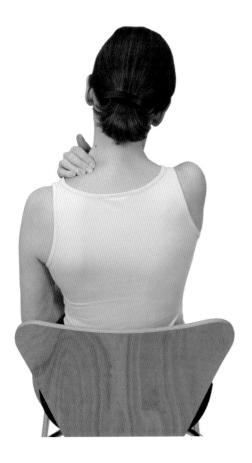

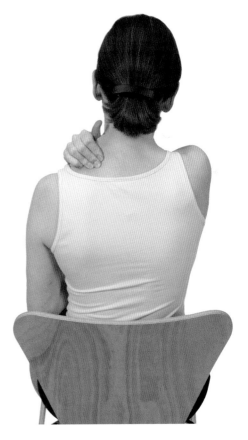

# enjoy nature

If you live in a noisy, overcrowded town or city, you may feel very detached from the natural world. You can bring many of its stress-relieving benefits into your life by exploring some of the options set out below.

- Spend as much time as possible outdoors: natural sunlight plays an important role in regulating the circadian rhythms that control sleep and hormone-production.

- Walk in the park: it gives you a break, takes you away from chores, and provides exercise. Notice the flowers planted for your enjoyment and let them transport you far from your troubles. Sometimes solutions to problems and hassles appear once you distance yourself from them.

- Jog on grass: as air is less polluted here than on roadside sidewalks, this reduces your toxic load. It also lessens risk of injury, and, being slightly more difficult, offers a more thorough workout.

- Opt for seaside or mountain vacations: more conducive to relaxation than city breaks unless you are a very energetic person. These are great places to meditate, if you can find a quiet spot.

- Visit gardens: the large number of beautiful gardens open to the public makes a relaxing alternative day out. Also visit lakes, woods, and other inspiring landscapes to take in the sights, sounds, and scents of nature.

- Create a shady arbor: if you have a garden, turn at least one corner into a pleasant place to sit and relax. Gardening is a rewarding pastime with visible rewards. As it involves physical work, it can help to release tension, and suits those who find it difficult to relax by sitting still.

- Nurture houseplants and window boxes: a good substitute for a garden. Keeping a plant on your desk helps counteract a sterile office atmosphere. Low-maintenance houseplant varieties include cacti, lithops (living stones), rubber plants, spider plants, cheese plants, ivy, geraniums, peace lilies, and streptocarpus.

- Grow herbs: basil, parsley, mint, and thyme thrive even on windowsills.

- Eat by the seasons: discovering and eating foods in season is an enjoyable way to feel more connected to the rhythms of nature. They have optimum taste, and may have traveled fewer miles from farm to store.

- Notice your mood patterns over the seasons: if the darker months leave you feeling down, you may be experiencing seasonal affective disorder (S.A.D.). Plenty of help is available, so don't be afraid to seek professional advice via your doctor.

- Care for pets: even small ones give you a sense of acceptance and help put your problems in proportion. They are valuable company for people who live alone. Stroking pets has been shown in studies to reduce heart rate and stress hormones.

# be creative

Everyone needs a regular interest outside of work and chores. Hobbies offer us the pleasure of being creative and act as an important diversion from the everyday worries and preoccupations that can get us down.

There are more benefits to be gained from positive leisure pursuits than from spending time watching television (although that in itself can sometimes be the perfect tonic after a stressful day). Most of us associate pastimes such as collecting stamps or playing an instrument with childhood, but these hobbies offer a valuable means of escape from a stressful work and home life. Pursuing an activity that's miles away from your line of work helps you forget about everything for a while.

Hobbies bring people together. If you never attempt a family bike ride, picnic, board game, or trip to the cinema you might never find out just how much fun it can be, and how much fun your family are too. Often outside interests broaden your horizons and lead to meeting new people as you learn new skills—you start by attending a foreign language course and end up with friends abroad.

Many hobbies guide you toward a slower pace of life. Bird-watching or photography require patience, and painting or embroidery are leisurely and thoughtful. The mind becomes absorbed, and racing thoughts slow down and feel more manageable.

Sometimes people are put off hobbies because they feel a need to achieve great results—to be the most talented painter or best pianist. But a hobby should be something you enjoy, whether or not it leads to praise from others. If it begins to feel like work, think about exploring another interest instead. The new talents you develop also have an impact on your confidence levels. Once you know that it's possible to learn to ride a horse or control a pair of skis, the impossible may suddenly seem within reach! If you don't have a hobby or interest, this just might be the right time to find one.

"You were intended not only to work, but to rest, laugh, play, and have proper leisure and enjoyment."

Grenville Kleiser

# stress-busting leisure pursuits

## reading
Attempt a book a week at home or join a book group—many local libraries hold regular reading groups. This pursuit suits those who prefer to be less extrovert.

## the theater
Watching a play can be stimulating as well as entertaining. Amateur dramatics provide a new social network and self-expression.

## travel
Exploring near or far broadens your horizons and experience and opens up all kinds of new possibilities. The self-sufficiency it entails is a boost for self-confidence.

## voluntary work
The opportunities to volunteer are endless and can be fitted into even the shortest amount of spare time.

## new sports
Try something you wouldn't usually attempt, such as ice-skating, badminton, or even go for the extreme—rock-climbing, hang-gliding, or bungee jumping.

## painting or sketching
Materials can be very cheap, and no-one has to look at what you've produced!

## writing
Keep a journal, pen poetry, try short stories or even shorter haikus. Or write that novel.

## organizing social events
Set up barbecues, coffee mornings, dinner parties, visits to museums, or go hill-walking with friends.

## puzzles
Mentally absorbing as well as physically relaxing. Attempt crosswords, jigsaw puzzles, quizzes, word searches, or number games.

## music
Take lessons or teach yourself, then consider joining up with others.

## astronomy
There may be a local group that offers lectures from visiting experts.

## collecting
Wine/dolls/rare records/thimbles, the choices are endless.

## evening classes
If you're sedentary all day try salsa dancing; if you work with your brain, try the hands-on creativity of pottery.

## gardening or flower arranging
Very therapeutic and allow for a good deal of creativity. Provide interaction with nature, the opportunity to learn new skills, and have beautifully tangible rewards.

## home brewing or winemaking
Enjoy making it; enjoy drinking it with friends.

## quilting, sewing, knitting, crochet
"The new yoga!" Especially good for those who prefer not to be physically active in their spare time. Also great when recuperating from an illness or time of stress.

## D.I.Y.
Be careful not to let it become a source of more stress!

# become self-aware

Our experience of stress depends on our reactions to the world around us. For this reason, self-awareness is a particularly valuable stress-management tool that allows us to understand our patterns of responses to events. Becoming aware of how you interact with others, and your desires, attitudes, and emotions, helps you take responsibility for both your successes and failures. Once you gain this knowledge, you can alter your reactions to stressful events as seems fit, and so reduce anxiety. Bringing the subconscious mind into consciousness allows you to act through choice, not in a blur of confusion.

Responses to stress vary, depending on the exact nature of the stress. Some people might find they work happily toward deadlines, but react badly to a noisy office or waiting in line. Once you figure out your own triggers, you can work on resolving them, or, at the very least, anticipating them. Use the opposite page to record what events trigger specific stress reactions in your life. If you find this exercise difficult, try making a note of your stress reactions soon after they occur, or at the end of each day. It might also be helpful to refer to your stress diary (see page 26).

## boosting your self-awareness

To become more self-aware, it's important to understand the key facets that make up your individuality, as set out below. Having a clear sense of who you are helps you decide what to do in any given situation, and will be of great benefit as the pressures mount.

## what makes me who I am?

### personality
Understand your personality and you'll learn to recognize which situations you thrive in and in which you struggle.

### priorities
It's easy to lose sight of priorities day-to-day. By focusing on them, you are more likely to achieve what you consider most important.

### tendencies
This means being aware of the habits you repeat regularly without thinking that reduce your effectiveness. For example, rushing headlong into an activity without realizing what it will involve.

### emotions
Understanding what causes feelings and how they affect your thoughts and actions is extremely valuable. People who are able to do this have an advantage in every area of life.

### needs
Some needs are shared by everyone, such as the demand for esteem, affection, belonging, achievement, and control. Individuals vary in which needs have most influence over them. Some people would rather have respect than be liked, others the opposite. When needs aren't met, they can cause frustration, conflict, and stress.

# my stress triggers and habitual responses

| stressful event or circumstance | my responses (actions and emotions) |
| --- | --- |
| Essay deadline. | Ignore it, then work through the night before it's due and do a bad job. Feel disappointed. |
| | |
| | |
| | |
| | |
| | |
| | |
| | |
| | |
| | |

## analyzing your results

It goes without saying that positive responses to stress need no more attention! Congratulate yourself on this, then turn your attention to the stress responses you are unhappy with. Can you find patterns? For example, perhaps they are the result of feeling anxious before meetings or jealous at social gatherings. Identifying emotions is often tough. Specific feelings can be difficult to separate from a general sense of anxiety. Often they are mixed up with beliefs and hopes. The emotion you feel consciously might be masking a different hidden emotion. Aim to keep an open mind, and not shy away from what is really going on.

The responses you show may be triggered by underlying issues. Hidden motivators for behavior include fear (of failure or loss), sadness (possibly due to bereavement), and anger (often with origins in the past).

above > **If you keep a stress diary, social gatherings may be revealed as an unexpected source of stress.**

The negative influence such problems can exert will continue until they are addressed. And when situations of high stress allow their effects to continue over time, we are put at greater risk of stress-related illness. Striving to be a high achiever is another common hidden source of motivation that forces many people to take on more than they can handle, resulting in stressful reactions. If you recognize this pattern in your own behavior, become aware of the tendency and ponder the consequences before saying yes next time. If you find it difficult to unravel your underlying motivations, try to explore them by writing a journal or talking with friends. If you feel it would be helpful, consult a counselor (see page 88).

# gain perspective

As stress builds up, we can lose our sense of perspective. It becomes hard to see the true significance of events, and thinking becomes distorted. Little annoyances feel huge, and sometimes the really important things, or people, get ignored. At such times it's impossible to see clearly the cause of stress, and easy to put the blame elsewhere. This is why it's essential to take breaks; to concentrate on something else, even for a short time. Once you regain perspective, you are better placed to decide on priorities for action. When you live a balanced life, giving your mind a rest from processing information every day, you are more able to focus on what you need to do when the time comes. The more accurate your perspective, the more chance you have of resolving your stress, or managing it well.

## how to do it

- Take time out: even five minutes will suffice.

- Talk things over with a friend: another time help him or her in return.

- Write down your thoughts: this forces you to impose some order on them.

- Take care of yourself: get enough sleep, eat well, and make time for fun, exercise, and relaxation.

below > **The beauty, serenity, and grandeur of nature can help you to put your own life into perspective.**

# use positive self-talk

The way we talk to ourselves determines our self-image and self-esteem. Positive self-talk can dramatically improve these important attributes. By calming your thoughts, you promote relaxation and reduce levels of stress hormones. This makes positive self-talk a powerful tool in your stress-management kit.

We tend to move toward whatever we set our sights on. So if we concentrate on what we don't have, we get less of what we want. If we focus on what's wrong, we won't find what's right. On the other hand, if we continually appreciate what's going well and expect a good result, we move in the right direction toward achieving it.

Negative self-talk is a habitual thought pattern and so is hard to break. If you find that you undermine yourself with negative self-talk, challenge this habit. Think of a situation in which your inner voice jeopardized your actions. Recall what you were telling yourself, what feelings this led to, and what actions you took. Then imagine a positive alternative.

In future, empower yourself by rewording negative statements into positives.

For example, if you regularly get cross with yourself for having an untidy house, stop seeing yourself as inadequate and think about a solution. Perhaps you are simply very busy and could give yourself the luxury of a cleaner once a week. Maybe you tell yourself that you're clumsy and useless when you accidentally break something. Instead, treat yourself with the same kindness that you would show to a friend. Each time you catch yourself making critical comments, fight back by using the following exercise. Practice the procedure during milder times of anxiety to start with so it becomes familiar during times of stress.

"Once I started to tell myself I deserved to be happier, it didn't take me long to believe it."

Andrew, a financial manager

## how to do it in a stress emergency

1 Stop the self-defeating thoughts—tell yourself at once that you are going to be positive.

2 Pause for a few moments. Close your eyes and concentrate on your breathing to help clear your mind.

3 Now fill your mind instead with positive thoughts and affirmations (see opposite).

4 Slowly open your eyes and return to the task in hand, taking it one step at a time.

## positive affirmations

These are statements used to "program" both the conscious and subconscious mind toward a better outcome. For each area of life you would like to work on, construct a short phrase that symbolizes the improvements you would like to take place. Repeat the phrase to yourself in your mind or out loud several times a day, and believe it. Look at the sample affirmations below, then try to put together some exactly suited to you. You might work them around specific examples—compliments you have received, your skills and talents, real achievements. Reading articles or books about joyful subjects can also be uplifting. Even thinking of small positive facts that might seem insignificant can help set you back on the right path.

### effective affirmations

I am working toward improving my life.

I am healthy, happy, and strong.

I am a valued and loveable person.

I have successful relationships.

I have the skills to do my job well.

I have worked hard to get where I am.

I have overcome many obstacles.

# build on your strengths

The philosopher Spinoza said that "to be what we are, and to become what we are capable of becoming, is the only end of life." Everyone has strengths—talents, skills, and competencies—but they vary from person to person. If we work with our strengths, we perform better, learn faster, and experience more enjoyment and fulfilment in life. The opposite is true when we focus on our weaknesses. Once you understand where your strengths lie, and use those skills, you will gain benefits in every area of life. And often you find your strengths compliment those of others when you work in a group.

To establish what your individual strengths are, fill in the table opposite. In the first column list each of your strong points, then use the right-hand column to record evidence to support your choices.

## types of strengths

• **Responsibility**

       • **Motivation**

• **Harmony**

       • **Experience**

• **Creativity**

       • **Commitment**

• **Empathy**

## how to identify your key strengths

• When are you happiest and most productive?

• Do you work better in a group or do you prefer to work by yourself?

• How do you see yourself react when someone approaches you with a work-related problem?

• What about a personal problem?

• How do you react to deadlines?

• What things do you choose to do in your leisure time?

"If at first you don't succeed, try again. Then quit. There is no point making a fool of yourself."

W.C. Fields

# my personal strengths

| strengths | supporting evidence |
|-----------|---------------------|
| Solidity | I feel happy and flattered that friends come to me for support and advice. |
| | |
| | |
| | |
| | |
| | |

## thinking about your results

- Make it a habit to step back from what you are doing and see if you can steer situations toward your strengths.

- Engage with your passions and find ways to realize your potential that incorporate your talents. This process might lead to a reassessment of what truly makes you happy; you may even begin to reconsider your priorities.

- As you build on your strengths, sometimes making progress and sometimes slipping back, take comfort from the fact that you are learning about yourself.

- If something isn't working, reassess.

# are you an introvert or extrovert?

Discovering this is just as important as identifying your strengths when learning about who you are and so being able to respond in times of stress from an informed and balanced perspective. You probably already know whether you are an introvert or an extrovert, but use the exercise below to challenge your assumptions.

## assessing your qualities

**1** Which are you most likely to do:

    **A** Think first and talk later.
    **B** Talk first and think later.

**2** On days off, which do you prefer?

    **A** Spending time reading or relaxing by yourself.
    **B** Spending time with friends or out shopping.

**3** How many good friends do you have?

    **A** One or two best friends.
    **B** Several best friends.

**4** When you're upset how do you react?

    **A** Keep it to yourself.
    **B** Talk to a friend about it.

## your results
Mainly **A** answers: you tend to be more introverted.
Mainly **B** answers: you veer toward extroversion.

## advice for introverts
Be aware that you may react to stress by becoming anxious or depressed. As you are in a minority, you may be put under pressure to change. Don't bow to this pressure; simply be yourself. If you need it, give yourself private, quiet time to recharge after interacting with others. You may need your own separate work space in order to be comfortable and productive. Use your strengths—a keen focus and concentration—and remember introverts frequently achieve great successes in life.

## advice for extroverts
You may tend to react to stress with impulsive and angry behavior. Be aware that you are more likely than an introverted person to resort to smoking and drinking in response to stressful situations, and that although you are better at communication than an introvert, you are also more easily distracted. Accept that you need others in order to refuel emotionally. Don't feel guilty about this or force yourself to try to deal with problems on your own. Try not to get frustrated with others who are less sociable and talkative.

Extrovert tendencies often manifest themselves
through impulsive behavior. Whether you're
introvert or extrovert, there's no right or wrong
way to be. You just need to learn how to manage
your personality.

# set goals

How do you plan your future? Some people drift more or less aimlessly from day to day and year to year without focusing on a long-term direction. Other people (the minority) set detailed goals and conform strictly to daily color-coded to-do lists! Most of us are in the middle, with hopes and dreams for the future, and either definite goals or a more vague plan of action. Usually people think hard about big decisions, but smaller ones tend to be driven more by mood and intuition. If you feel you would benefit, take the time each day to set specific goals and determine what you want to achieve. Below are some tips on ways to set and accomplish goals. Once you have digested these, try to complete the goal-planner chart set out opposite, and update it often. The sample plan, for instance, would need updating weekly. Your plan might need updating more or less often.

## how to do it

### choose the right goals

Try to find the middle ground between aiming too high and not high enough. Aiming high is a good motivator, but if you don't feel the goal is attainable, you'll be put off even trying. Bear in mind both your ability and your enthusiasm. Importantly, think hard about why you want to achieve the goal. Is the result going to be worth the investment? When choosing a goal, it's useful to think along these lines: Is it challenging, valuable, specific, measurable, and does it have a specific deadline? Some goals are continuous and so won't meet all the guidelines, for example, increasing the amount you recycle. Overall, a good goal is one that is worthy of your time and effort, and that, in the end, can only be your decision.

### make it formal

Writing down a goal seems to make it official and adds to your sense of commitment. It might also be effective to share your idea with one or two friends. Imagine yourself having achieved the goal.

### devise a plan

This is vital to make the goal a reality. Without a plan, it has little chance of success. Write an overall summary of the goal, including details such as timing, cost, and location to make it feel authentic. Decide where to begin, and then make a detailed step-by-step plan of the major tasks needed to achieve the goal. If in doubt, work backward in stages from the final result. Make deadlines if you like, but keep them realistic to prevent disappointment.

### stick to it

This is the biggest challenge. Finding a good time to start often holds the process back. There will never be a perfect time; goals just have to fit into your lifestyle. Unexpected events can distract you and lead to procrastination, but maintain your motivation. Keep at the front of your mind the happiness you will feel on achieving your goal. If possible, report back to others on your progress. The plan also needs to be flexible enough to adjust as you go along.

# goal planner chart

| | plan to reach my goals | | |
|---|---|---|---|
| goal | To lose five pounds with minimum effort. | | |
| motivation | To feel comfortable on vacation in bikini. | | |
| resources | Healthy food Running shoes | | |
| time-scale | Vacation 10 weeks away. | | |
| steps needed | Run 30 minutes twice a week. Reduce junk food and alcohol. | | |
| sub-goals | To lose 1 pound every 2 weeks. | | |
| starting date | Tomorrow | | |
| aims this week | Run on Tuesday and Thursday. Food shopping on Monday. | | |
| potential problems | Birthday meal on Wednesday. | | |

**regularly reassess**

Frequently reexamine the goal to ensure it's still what you really want. Recognize and celebrate each small success along the way. Adapt the goal, if necessary, but keep to your main objective. Work hard and stay focused on the result.

# establish priorities

If you are good at setting priorities, you will be better prepared to make decisions about goals, and in so doing, manage stress. Stressful situations often force us instantly to prioritize commitments and decide which matters can be safely put to one side for a while and which can't. Under pressure, some aspects of life inevitably become less urgent than others. But be sure not to entirely ignore any one area. This could be the part that keeps you sane! Let priorities evolve as the need arises. On a daily level, to-do lists can help organize your schedule according to the importance of each activity. Use stars, arrows, numbers, or letters, or devise your own system. Of course, it's tempting to put the least painful task first, but think how pleased you'll be when the nasty ones are complete!

## how to prioritize daily activities

1 Make a system of lists or in-trays that code items by importance.

2 In the top tray, or at the top of the list, grade urgent items that require immediate attention.

3 In the center tray, or middle of the list, place things that require attention in the near future.

4 Finally, use the bottom tray or at the bottom of the sheet of paper, for non-essential or non-urgent affairs.

## prioritizing tips

- **Learn to say no to people who try to make you change your agenda against your wishes.**

- **Allow some margin for unpredictable interruptions and delays.**

- **Plan to maximize your sense of accomplishment while creating space for relaxation too.**

right > In a pressurized lifestyle, it is easy to forget to make time for relaxation. It is essential to balance your life and set time aside for activities you enjoy.

# manage your time

We all have 24 hours in a day, yet some of us feel we don't have enough time to get things done while others achieve all their goals and still fit in fun and relaxation. The effects of poor time management can reduce productivity and contribute to many stress-related problems. If you underestimate the time it takes to complete tasks, you add unnecessary stress to your day. Underestimating the time an early-morning task will take can throw off the schedule for the rest of the day, and may even have a negative impact on the following few days. The solution is to allocate sufficient time, plus a bit extra. Here's how.

Predicting how much time a task will take is difficult for many people. Those who have type-A tendencies (see page 16), people under pressure from tight deadlines, perfectionists and procrastinators all have particular problems giving themselves enough time for tasks. If you are in the habit of pushing yourself too hard because you have unrealistic expectations and standards,

time-management skills not only help you avoid these hassles, but work as a valuable stress-management tool, too. The effort involved will be worth it for the sense of accomplishment. When chores are either done or allotted a dedicated slot, the quality of your sleep and relaxation time improves, too. First assess your current time-management skills by asking yourself some telling questions.

## how effective is your current time management?

- **Do you have enough time to do the things you enjoy?**

- **Are you constantly rushing and often late?**

- **Do you often cancel social activities because you're too busy?**

- **Do you feel as if there are not enough hours in the day?**

- **Do you become frustrated and impatient?**

**analyzing your answers**
The way in which you respond to these questions might highlight a need to look at how you divide your time and whether your current method is working. To do so, you need to recognize your needs and allocate time in a balanced way. Lack of balance can lead to burnout. Effective time management involves thinking about your activities and planning how to make the most of this valuable resource.

"Nature does not hurry, yet everything is accomplished."

Lao Tzu, Chinese Taoist philosopher

## how happy are you with the amount of time spent in the following areas?

- Work: time spent working (paid or voluntary).

- Home: time spent on regular household tasks, maintenance, and gardening.

- Social life: time with other people, including children, friends, and family.

- Personal life: includes time devoted to hobbies, relaxation, exercise, and sleep.

- Private life: time with your partner.

- "Me-time": time alone thinking and reflecting.

### analyzing your answers

If you are not happy with the amount of time you spend on any one area, think of ways to reallocate your time. Consider which activities you would like to spend more or less time on, and how you could make this happen. Perhaps you could reduce the amount of work you take home, or organize a more effective laundry system. If you find it hard to know how much time you spend on each task, it might be helpful to keep a written record of how you fill up each hour over a week. At the end of the week you will have a much clearer idea of where your time goes. Then work on the chart below.

## my ideal time plan

### I would like to spend more time on:

1 ...........................................................................................................................

2 ...........................................................................................................................

3 ...........................................................................................................................

### I would like to spend less time on:

1 ...........................................................................................................................

2 ...........................................................................................................................

3 ...........................................................................................................................

### Ways to achieve this new balance:

1 ...........................................................................................................................

2 ...........................................................................................................................

3 ...........................................................................................................................

## list-making

Make lists when you feel overwhelmed: deadlines, work, and personal tasks always seem more organized on paper. Simply writing the list gives the impression that you have already begun to conquer it. Start the list with an easy task to get you going. But beware the oppressive power of the list and remember who's in charge of it! If an item has been carried over from many previous lists, cross it off—it can't be that necessary or appealing.

## managing time at work

To keep track of your daily tasks, try out checklists, sticky notes, diaries, calendars, personal or electronic organizers, and appointment books among many other methods. Time at work is often lost because of disorganized filing drawers, lack of an in-tray system, unnecessary copies of paperwork, and colleagues with a hoarding instinct.

In meetings, when they drag on, aim to steer conversation back to the matter in hand and sum up progress made so far. If you feel it's appropriate, point out the time.

Keep phone calls to a minimum—they can continue longer than expected. Explain that you have an urgent task to complete, and, if appropriate, suggest a better time to talk.

If you work from home, set up systems for filing and making appointments. Ensure that computer data is backed up regularly to avoid loss of information. The more frequently you backup information, the less disruption is likely should an accident happen and data be lost.

## using peak-performance times

Body-clocks vary between individuals, and we all have times of day at which we feel more and less energetic. Some people get most done in the morning; others don't feel alert until late afternoon. This can have an effect on time management. As far as possible, take on more demanding tasks when you have maximum energy.

right > **We all have different body clocks, and learning when you function best is an important part of managing your life and stress levels.**

"If I have a lot to do, I much prefer to get into the office early than stay late. My mind works better in the mornings."

Richard, lawyer

# be confident

The dictionary definition of confidence is "a state of being self-assured and feeling or showing self-reliance." We could all benefit from a little more of this in at least one area of life. Most of us are confident in one arena, but less so in others. Perhaps you are comfortable in social groups but shy at work, or vice versa. Many people are extremely confident around people they know, but feel awkward meeting strangers, or you may be one of those very quiet souls who gets a kick from public speaking. Low confidence can lead to feelings of anxiety, helplessness, and stress, and situations in which you feel powerless—such as losing your job—give confidence the greatest knock. Becoming more confident requires you to focus on your strengths, skills, and abilities. If you are aware of the resources you have, and how to apply them, you can be strong and optimistic in the face of life's challenges.

## how satisfied are you with your current level of self-confidence?

To begin assessing how confident you are, spend a few minutes thinking about the following questions:

- **Do you feel comfortable making small talk with strangers?**

- **Do you participate fully in meetings?**

- **Can you pick up on other people's body language?**

- **Can you relax in unfamiliar situations?**

- **How do you react to conflict?**

- **Do you know where your strengths lie?**

- **Can you easily move on from a failure?**

**analyzing your answers**

Consider why these situations are currently so difficult, and think about which of your talents and strengths you could use to counter them. Visualize yourself being assertive in all areas of life, and calculate the practical actions you could take toward this more constructive way of being.

### why increase your confidence?

Increasing your confidence takes time, but is worth every minute. Think about the reasons why you want to build your confidence, and imagine what you could achieve. Now list three areas of your life where greater confidence would be useful (for example, when you are talking to a patronizing colleague).

# what makes true confidence?

### self-presentation
The way in which you present yourself includes positive body language and making a good first impression.

### perception
You know you have this when you find it easy to recognize and respond to other people's feelings and moods.

### awareness of feelings
This is not only about being in touch with your emotions, but also understanding what drives your actions.

### ability to take charge
You are capable of identifying opportunities and going for it with the aim of maximizing your success.

# tips to increase confidence

- Notice your patterns of actions, emotions, and thoughts: decide which of these are helpful and which you would rather jettison. Make a concerted effort to leave the negative patterns you have developed behind and move on. This includes ridding yourself of destructive self-talk.

- Take inspiration from people you admire.

- Be well prepared for events that are likely to test your confidence.

- Practice small-talk skills with people you are comfortable with: before social gatherings, equip yourself with conversation topics to fall back on if necessary. If in doubt, ask other people open-ended questions about themselves.

- If you feel awkwardly self-conscious, try to distract yourself by concentrating very hard on something else.

- Remember no-one is better or more valuable than you.

# communicate effectively

Using good communication skills—expressing yourself clearly and listening well—can often help to avoid or reduce stress. Unfortunately, we are more likely to communicate ineffectively under stress, just at the time when we most need to get assistance from others. Tension itself often arises from interaction with other people, when a hiccup in communication is likely to trigger stressful consequences. When we rush, we are less likely to keep others fully up-to-date, and often fail to listen properly because we are preoccupied with other tasks. But when ideas and attitudes are effectively communicated, we find ourselves in a win-win situation in every sphere of life. This can prevent unnecessary misunderstandings and consequent tensions within the family at home, at work, and during social events.

## how to do it

- Try to open up channels of communication as much as possible.

- Actively make time to talk with your partner and children: look for opportunities such as when driving or washing up.

- Make extra effort on important days: the high expectations that accompany vacations and holidays can make little things seem much more significant.

- Act promptly: deal with problems as soon as they arise.

- Try harder when relationships seem tense: make a conscious effort to practise the basic communication skills of listening and expressing yourself.

# basic communication skills

## listening

Effective listening calls for concentration, tolerance, and sensitivity. Concentration means focusing solely on what the speaker is saying. Tolerance involves keeping an open mind to what the other person is saying, rather than being judgmental or defensive. Sensitivity encompasses taking on board the feelings being expressed as well as the words. When under stress, you are likely to be more preoccupied than usual and fail to listen well. It's a good habit to ask a speaker to repeat what he or she said if you doubt that you fully understood it. If you're a good listener, you will probably be kept better informed.

## expressing yourself

First you need to be sure of what you want to get across. When you feel confused, spend a few quiet moments mulling over your thoughts. Then you'll be ready to state your message clearly, honestly, and constructively. Avoid negative generalizations about the other person. In arguments, attempt to stay on the topic that is the real problem and avoid point-scoring and venting anger just to calm yourself down. Positive resolutions don't come from attacking. Learn when to give feedback and how to say no to unreasonable demands from people.

## reading body language

By its very nature, it's difficult to explain body language, or non-verbal communication, in words. However, it's important to understand that it is a key form of communication. Through clues in another person's movements, it is possible to pick up signs about how your message is being received. We pick up on these clues all the time without realizing it, perhaps ignoring the messages.

When you are talking, look out for signs of understanding, distraction, confusion, or even boredom in the listener, and adapt your behavior in response. Be aware of crossed arms and avoidance of eye contact—if you see this happening, you might need to alter your approach completely.

## being aware of difference

Individuals' perceptions of the same event or piece of information can vary a great deal. Different backgrounds lead to varying expectations of the world, and we tend to hear what we expect to hear. Put yourself in other people's shoes and gear your message toward the listener. Make sure your meaning has been received accurately by asking for feedback. Also remember that many words have different definitions and so often lay themselves open to misinterpretation.

left > **Making an extra effort on important family days pays dividends—significant occasions such as birthdays provide rare time out from a demanding lifestyle to show loved ones how much you care.**

## resolving conflict

Whenever people are working or living in close proximity, there are times at which conflicts arise, even with the best of intentions. Clashes can arise in many ways, including because people have different standards or beliefs. Arguments can also arise simply because someone arrived in the office in a bad mood. Human interaction is what brings the greatest satisfactions—and sometimes the greatest tensions—to a working environment.

Conflict, in fact, has the potential to be useful and can be channeled in healthy ways as long as it doesn't involve threats or excessive stubbornness. Combat can stimulate discussion and bring people closer together if everyone involved expresses his or her feelings and opinions in an open way.

Resolve conflicts by working together in a manner in which no one is forced to give in to, or be dominated by, anyone else. Look for solutions that are acceptable to everyone, and keep working at it until all parties feel satisfied.

## communicating well at work

In the workplace, effective communication is the key to success. At work most of us have to communicate with a wide range of people, including managers, colleagues, customers, and the general public. Ineffective communication can affect working relationships and even jeopardize chances of promotion. Equally, good communication can greatly increase job satisfaction and improve your performance.

Business experts believe the success of an organization derives from the quality of the human decision-making within it. Good communication can motivate others to act on your decisions.

When communicating by email, phone, text, memo, or letter, ask yourself, "Can this message be easily understood by the person receiving it?" Decide on your goal and choose appropriate language to help you achieve it. Keep it focused for greater chance of success.

"Departmental meetings don't just allow us to go through our schedules. They're a crucial opportunity for my staff and I to chat and get things off our chest."

**Tracy, departmental manager**

# plan to resolve conflict

| point of conflict | resolution | outcome |
| --- | --- | --- |
| | | |
| | | |
| | | |
| | | |
| | | |

# build social support

"No man is an island, entire of itself," wrote John Donne in 1624. The message is just as relevant today. Men and women are social beings, and we depend on each other for everything from food and healthcare to love and support. People with a strong social-support network show fewer symptoms of stress and are less likely to become ill as a result of stress. They also tend to live longer. On the other hand, people who are isolated with no one to confide in have a higher rate of illness. We need supportive friends as well as a partner—one person cannot provide a wide enough range of interaction. Significant events, such as anniversaries and birthdays, have so much more meaning when shared with loving relatives and friends. Today, even the internet can help us avoid isolation. There are online forums covering all interests—you can even play games against opponents on the other side of the world!

## "I feel most connected with others when I go out with my girlfriends."

Janet, business journalist

## being supported through stress

Social support is most helpful at times of stress. Talking about feelings reduces tension, helps you work through problems, and allows you to feel better about yourself. Sharing difficult times brings you closer to others as you give and receive comfort, reassurance, advice, and distraction, and make each other laugh. Other people can also provide practical help, such as collecting children from school or shopping for food. They could show you how to use a computer, or help you write a C.V. in a last-minute emergency.

Support groups, such as Alcoholics Anonymous, exist for almost every problem and illness. People who are part of a support group, with its sense of welcome, acceptance, and understanding, have been shown to do better than those who suffer alone. To find a group that suits you, see the resources information on page 154–157

Words of encouragement or consolation from people who are important to us really help us overcome adversity, so don't be shy of opening up. Confide only what you're comfortable with—you don't have to divulge every last detail. Most importantly, don't see yourself as weak for seeking support. We all feel stressed, angry, frustrated, or scared at times. It's a mistake to keep those feelings locked within. Having problems simply means you're human. Remember the adage "A problem shared is a problem halved."

## how to build a support network

- Don't be shy of contacting old friends or workmates: even if you haven't heard from them in years, pick up the telephone or send them an email.

- Widen your social circle: take advantage of new opportunities when they arise. Look for volunteer work, evening classes, sports teams, or community groups that match your interests. Or start your own support group, for example, on stress management!

above > **Your relationships provide an essential support system in times of crisis and you should never be afraid to ask for help from the people who love you.**

- Make it clear to friends that you're available: take an interest in their lives and be willing to support them in return.

- Nurture a wide social circle: include friends you can spend time with whether you're feeling happy, sad, relaxed, or lively.

# seek counseling

If you need more support than you are willing to ask for from friends and family, you might consider seeing a counselor. These pages explain what is involved and set out the different types of counseling available.

## what is counseling?

A counselor is a trained outside observer who can provide support and advice and may be able to offer a new perspective that helps you get to the root of any serious problems. Counseling is now very popular, and most family doctors can offer appointments or referrals. Many thousands more counselors work privately.

The concerns that people bring to counseling are widely varied, but include work-related and relationship difficulties; feelings of depression, anxiety, anger, and bereavement; traumatic incidents and childhood abuse; eating disorders and problems of addiction. However you do not need to be in crisis to have counseling (although this is often a good

## questions to ask

What kind of counseling do you offer and what is its aim?

Can I contact you between sessions if I need to?

How many sessions might I need and how does the counseling end?

time to focus on problems). Counseling can offer preventative care if you are able to recognize when you are beginning to feel anxious and troubled.

The counseling process helps you cope with and identify the sources of your stress as well as develop solutions to it. Counseling enhances self-confidence and tends to be more successful in the short-term if it concentrates on a specific problem. Some mild stress-related ailments improve after the cause of the symptoms has been explained and dealt with. Many people who suffer from anxiety or depression benefit from counseling, learning coping strategies to help work through their problems.

How many years have you been practicing?

Have you had experience of working with people with similar problems to mine?

## what happens at a session?

Counseling sessions take place in a private room, and you usually sit in a chair facing the counselor. Sessions tend to last 50 minutes to an hour and they can be arranged for couples and groups as well as individuals.

The counselor will start by asking you about your problems and background. Use the first session to ensure that you are happy talking to this person. If you don't feel comfortable with the counselor after a few sessions, he or she may not be the right person for you. If the relationship is productive, you will be able to vent your feelings and possibly get years of emotional pain off your chest. It will provide a safe, confidential environment in which you can speak freely to someone who will listen attentively and without passing judgment.

Through counseling you can explore your thoughts, feelings, and concerns. It will help you establish the origins of your feelings and look at how your past affects your current state of affairs. You should in time establish a clearer understanding of what led you to suffer from a particular problem, start thinking about how you may be repeating patterns of behavior, and learn to view yourself in a more positive light.

## how long will it continue?

This is a very individual question—some people need fewer sessions, and some people require more. This can be reviewed as the counseling proceeds. Progress can be slow and sometimes painful whichever approach is used. The success of counseling usually owes more to the relationship between you and your counselor, than to the theoretical approach.

## which type of counseling?

There are no clear answers as to which kind of
therapy is best for different people or different
types of problems. Modern counseling offers a
range of approaches, the main ones being
cognitive, behavioral, and psychoanalytic.
Cognitive and behavioral approaches help you
examine the ways in which you think and
behave. In so doing, they aim to change the
way you feel. The psychoanalytic approach
looks at possible childhood causes of current
feelings. Many counselors use a combination
of the two approaches.

### cognitive therapy
Looks for negative thought patterns which
may be unconscious, and aims to adjust them
into more positive ways of approaching the
world. The assumption is that negative
thoughts produce negative emotions. This
approach works well for depression.

### behavioral therapy
Aims to identify the triggers that cause
unproductive behavior and anxiety, and
focuses on how to change that behavior. This
approach is effective for anxiety disorder, and
panic attacks. It focuses less on the thought
patterns behind the behavior.

right > **There are many types of counseling available,
but don't forget the importance of talking to a friend.**

### psychoanalytic therapy

Helps you look back into the past to discover unconscious conflicts. It is less interactive than the cognitive and behavioral approaches, and the counselor does not offer advice. The client is encouraged to explore thoughts, perceptions, and behaviors without judgment. It is important to remain focused on the goal in this approach.

### other approaches

Some counselors use hypnotism, especially when working with phobias, fears, habitual behavior, anxiety, and stress. This is generally most successful as a long-term treatment. There are also more specific types of counseling for defined problems, focusing on areas such as anger management, assertiveness training, sexual or marital problems, addictions, disabilities, and bereavement.

## finding a counselor

Choosing a counselor can be daunting, but there are so many out there that, in the end, you are sure to find one who suits you. If you don't feel comfortable after a few sessions, leave and try out another counselor. The relationship between you and the counselor is vital to the success of the process. Your doctor may be able to refer you to a counselor or recommend one. Refer also to the resources on page 154–157. Any counselor who is registered with a professional association will have had appropriate training and will follow proper guidelines.

# eat well

Stress and food go hand-in-hand for most of us. Food can give us the feelings of power, control, and satisfaction we need to survive stressful situations. It is no surprise that as our stress levels go up, our resistance to "comfort" foods declines. This isn't always a bad thing—favorite foods can actually reduce stress levels, but, as always, moderation is the key to good health and a balanced state of mind.

Giving your body the nutrition it needs is a positive step you can take every day toward combating stress. Armed with the correct nutrients, you are best prepared to face the challenges of the day. Eating a sensible, balanced diet also reduces the effects of stress on the body and helps deter common digestive problems, such as indigestion and cravings, thus protecting your health.

Some people eat more under stress; others eat less. Whichever type you are, this is a sign that you do not prioritize healthy eating when the pressure is on, the very time that you most need good nutrients and yet fast food and comfort foods have most appeal for you. During stressful periods, the body produces adrenaline, a process which uses up energy stores. This ensures an energy burst in an emergency, but soon after causes blood sugar levels to drop. Sustaining food is needed to replenish them. Certain foods increase the physical stress on your body by making digestion more difficult or by denying the brain essential nutrients. Drinks can have just as great an effect—caffeine and alcohol put considerable strain on the body, and sometimes the mind, too. Add on the fact that stress in itself can lead to digestive difficulties and it becomes clear that this aspect of life benefits greatly from a little attention. Try some of the suggestions below to counter digestive problems associated with stress.

## avoiding stress-related digestive problems

### indigestion
This can result from eating in the middle of a stressful situation, when your digestive system is not relaxed. It can also be caused by eating on the run. To prevent it, ensure you sit down for meals and eat more slowly, chewing food properly. You will then really taste and enjoy both meals and snacks.

### bloating
As we all know, bloating is unpleasant and stressful in itself! It can be triggered by wheat products (bread, pasta, cakes, and cookies) and dairy products (milk, cheese, butter, and cream), so try cutting out each food group for a couple of weeks to see if the problem eases. (If you are pregnant, breastfeeding, or have a health condition, consult your doctor or dietician before excluding food groups.)

### caffeine dependency
Relying on caffeine to keep you going is not a good idea. It raises the production of stress hormones and can lead to insomnia and

dehydration, impacting on your body's ability to handle stress. Substitute the many delicious caffeine-free alternatives, such as herbal teas.

above > **A healthy diet is essential to good management of stress.**

## hangovers

No-one functions at their best with a hangover, so drinking heavily always leads to trouble the following day. This does not mean that you need avoid alcohol completely, just be aware of its effects, and resist using it as a coping technique (too often!).

## cravings

These often hit during the "post-lunch dip," and increase at hormonal times and in the face of stress. To curb cravings, include small portions of the craved item in your usual diet rather than trying to resist completely. Or distract yourself by getting involved in another activity; the craving may pass. Keep healthy food nearby, and do not leave too many hours between snacks.

## sugar highs and lows

Although the brain needs glucose to enable it to perform effectively, very sugary foods cause blood sugar levels to shoot up and then drop, leaving you feeling sleepy and lethargic. This can lead to another sweet craving, and so the cycle continues.

# the basics of good nutrition

Rather than thinking in terms of "good" and "bad" foods, give thought to the overall balance of your food intake over a day, making sure you include something from all the main food groups, as described below. Most meals can be adapted to these proportions without compromising on taste. For example, you can use more pasta and less meat in a lasagne, or grill foods instead of frying. Get into the habit of adding a few more vegetables to a dish, and keeping an eye on the fat and sugar. Many types of cooking, such as Thai cuisine, are naturally low in fat and high in fiber. The strong flavors make up for the lack of oil, butter or cream, so be adventurous! A diet that includes a wide variety of foods will be more interesting as well as more likely to give your body what it needs.

## carbohydrates

Bread, other cereals, and potatoes provide the body with energy, vitamins, minerals, and fiber, and should make up a third of your daily intake. Ideal sources include wholemeal bread, brown rice, wholewheat pasta, rye, porridge oats, and baked potatoes.

## fruit and vegetables

Should also comprise a third of your daily intake. This group provides vitamins and fiber. Aim for at least five portions a day, for instance, one apple, two plums, three dried apricots, a good helping of vegetables, and one glass of fruit or vegetable juice.

## dairy produce

Milk and dairy foods should make up one-sixth of your daily food intake. They contain calcium, protein, and some vitamins, making them vital for growth and repair.

## protein

Meat, fish, and alternative sources of protein should constitute just over 10 percent of your daily intake. They provide iron, protein, vitamins, and minerals. Eggs, beans, soya products, tofu, nuts, and seeds fit into this food group.

## fat and sugar

Should make up just under 10 percent of your daily intake. Some fats are better than others. Steer clear of saturated fats, mainly found in meat products, and trans fats as in hydrogenated vegetable oil or fat. Polyunsaturated and monounsaturated fats, from olive, walnut, sesame, sunflower, or safflower oils are preferable.

# how to improve your diet through the day

## breakfast

Always eat breakfast, even if you can only manage a piece of fruit. A great choice for breakfast is a fruit smoothie. Make them with various combinations of fruit, including oranges, grapefruit, apricots, peaches, bananas, mangoes, and pineapple, with or without live natural yogurt. Be adventurous by adding vegetables, such as carrot or red peppers, and spice it up with cinnamon, vanilla, ginger, and nutmeg.

## lunch and evening meal

Healthy options include baked potatoes with cheese or tuna, sushi, vegetable soup, wholemeal sandwiches, or salads. In restaurants, baked fish or chicken with vegetables is always a good choice. Or opt for pasta with a tomato-based sauce.

## in-between

Snack on healthy food throughout the day for sustained energy. This calls for a little planning—carry with you a banana, yogurt, nuts and raisins, a few oatcakes, or a bagel.

## drinks

Cut down on stimulants like coffee, tea, and sodas as much as you can. Substitute decaffeinated coffee or tea, fruit juices, and herbal teas. Drink plenty of water (at least eight glasses a day) to prevent dehydration and protect your kidneys.

## alcohol

Sadly, alcohol supplies little or no nutrients. Women should consume less than seven units of alcohol a week; men 14 units (one unit is a small glass of wine or half pint of beer). Attempt to match each alcoholic drink with a glass of water or fruit juice.

## supplements

Consider vitamin and mineral supplements to replace the nutrients used up by stress reactions, particularly B vitamins, vitamin C, calcium, magnesium, and zinc. Herbal supplements that aid digestion include licorice root, aloe vera, lemongrass, and kava kava. Some teas are helpful to digestion: try mint, dandelion, fennel, ginger, slippery elm, and meadowsweet.

**please note**

If you are pregnant, breastfeeding, or taking prescribed medication for any medical condition, consult your doctor, nutritionist, or herbalist before taking herbal and nutritional supplements. If these restrictions do not apply, take the dose suggested on the bottle.

# get quality sleep

Quality sleep is essential, but virtually all of us have trouble sleeping during periods of stress. If you have difficulty in falling asleep, are woken during the night, or wake early in the morning, get comfort from knowing you're not alone. Regular lack of sleep causes concentration, mood, and energy levels to suffer. This reduces effectiveness at work and patience with family, and so can lead to more stress. Try some of the ideas below to ensure sweet dreams every night.

## Strategies which may help to improve the quality of your sleep:

### good sleep "hygiene"

- Stick to a regular routine as far as possible: don't be tempted to sleep in late at weekends.

- Try to spend at least 30 minutes a day outside: daylight is a powerful regulator of the body clock.

- Take regular exercise: this is one of the best sleep aids, so try to workout every day. You will see other benefits too.

- Avoid caffeine in the evening. Avoid nicotine, too, as much as possible, both being addictive stimulants that keep you awake. Caffeine is found in coffee, tea, cocoa, cola, and chocolate.

- Eat a light dinner at least two hours before going to bed: any later and your stomach will be too busy digesting to allow you to sleep well. Sleep-inducing bedtime drinks include warm milk or camomile tea.

- Keep alcohol to a minimum: indulging may send you to sleep quickly, but will dehydrate you, interrupting your sleep later on.

- Do something to relax: before going to bed have a warm bath; listen to quiet music, or do a relaxation exercise (see page 48). Be peaceful for the hour before you go to bed and your body will unwind.

- Instigate a specific "worry time": several hours before going to bed complete your "to-do" lists to empty your mind. Also avoid working, studying, or watching scary movies before bedtime.

**A good night's sleep makes a crucial difference to your waking life, and a warm bath in the evening prepares your mind and body for wind down.**

## In the bedroom

- Keep the bedroom cosy: make it quiet, dark, and uncluttered. Wear soft, cosy nightwear, and ensure the bed is comfortable.

- Leave the bedroom if you are unable to sleep: it's best to get up and do something relaxing, such as reading. Go back to bed when you feel sleepy. You may need to repeat this process, but don't watch a clock or you may start to panic about not sleeping, making it less likely that you will.

- Try herbal remedies: valerian, passiflora, and kava kava have a good reputation (avoid during pregnancy and while breastfeeding; do not combine valerian with conventional sleep medication). Up to 10 drops of lavender essential oil in the bath can work well (avoid during the first trimester of pregnancy). The flower remedies passion flower, hops, orange blossom, and Scot's pine might also help.

- Keep cool in summer: on a hot night open windows and doors to create a draft. Remove quilts and blankets, and wear light cotton nightwear, if anything. Take a cool shower or bath before going to bed. Use a fan if necessary.

- Stay warm in winter: keep the bedroom warm but not too hot, and block any draughts. Have a warm bath and a warm drink just before bed. Hot water bottles and electric blankets can make all the difference.

- Last resort: if you have to use sleeping pills, make sure they do not interact with any other medication. Use the lowest dose and never mix with alcohol.

# summary

- Everyone benefits from building stress-reducing activities, such as exercise, relaxation, and hobbies, into their lives.

- Eating well and ensuring you have sufficient rest and sleep prepares you to ride the inevitable stresses of life.

- The way you talk to yourself is crucial to self-esteem; avoid making critical comments.

- Being aware of your priorities, strengths, and needs gives you the ability to plan and work toward goals.

- Taking the time to communicate effectively makes a big difference under stress.

- Friends, family, and organized groups are an enormous source of stress-relief. Don't keep it all locked up!

- Counseling can be a great way to get to the root of problems and overcome them.

# notes

# chapter 3

# stress-reducing programs

# emergency techniques

"The time to relax is when you don't have time for it," said the wise American journalist Sydney J. Harris. Some of the most important stress-management techniques are those you can apply on the spot when you feel stress levels rising.

## stress-relieving formulas

- Take a break: remove yourself from the situation, if necessary, inventing an excuse so you can spend a few moments by yourself. You will be able to think more clearly and get in touch with your feelings. Then decide what to do to lift the pressure.

- Breathe deeply and slowly for a few minutes: this provides extra oxygen for physical and emotional wellbeing. (In fact the word "inspiration" derives from the breathing process.) If you are able, use the simple breathing exercise from page 50.

- Eat regularly: to prevent headaches and energy dips go for low-sugar foods and avoid caffeine. Try not to miss meals, however unimportant they seem.

## on-the-spot relaxation

1 Close your eyes and take 10 long, deep breaths in and out. Empty your mind of all intrusive thoughts.

2 Imagine yourself on a peaceful and sunny desert island or other calm location, just for a moment. This can do wonders in drawing your mind away from the causes of your stress.

- Use calming essential oils: place 2 drops of essential oil of lavender or jasmine on a handkerchief and inhale (avoid during pregnancy). Drink camomile tea, or look for a herbal tea containing valerian (avoid this if using sleep medication).

- Ask for help: delegate or share responsibility. Often those around you won't realize how overloaded you're feeling. Don't worry about looking as if you can't cope to others; on the contrary, you'll appear organized and forward-thinking.

- Renegotiate: if a deadline looks unrealistic, don't just struggle on.

- Go for a ten minute walk: or sit in the park for a while, perhaps with a book or music.

- Have a warm and relaxing bubble bath.

- Write down your thoughts: then they begin to make sense. Make decisions about priorities and look for solutions. Even if it feels like a hassle, it will be worth it. There's almost always a way of making things easier. Try to be detached and take a step back. Think creatively—what would someone else do in your situation?

"I close my eyes and take a few deep breaths. A minute or two is all it takes to calm down."

**Shelley, an interpreter**

- Don't try to control the uncontrollable: instead adapt by changing your response.

- Take lunch breaks and leave work on time: you'll be more effective when your energy is topped up.

- Do one thing at a time: this might take conscious effort. Avoid worrying about the next task to come. Use a to-do list, wall planner, or other organizational aid.

- Reduce your standards: if only temporarily. Never aim to do something absolutely perfectly, it will only lead to frustration.

- Meet up with supportive friends: let off steam, then listen to their problems and you'll begin to feel more sane. They might offer solutions you hadn't thought of.

- Ask someone to rub your shoulders or back.

- Book a day off or a vacation: just daydreaming about it will help. When the time comes, don't fill up the hours with D.I.Y. or other chores.

- Consciously choose to view situations in a positive light: use constructive self-talk (see page 66) to cultivate a positive frame of mind. After all, some stress is necessary for us to stay sharp and do our best. Albert Einstein said, "In the middle of difficulty lies opportunity."

- Try to see the funny side: this is not always possible, but keep amusing emails/cards in your purse to turn to at stressful times. Recall recent times when you've laughed out loud.

- Plan a treat: a massage or manicure, perhaps, or schedule in some "me-time" when no-one is allowed to disturb you. A trip to the cinema or theater should guarantee no interruptions.

- Get engrossed: sometimes the best way to unwind is to do something just as stimulating. Try an activity that involves your energy and/or full concentration, but uses a different part of the brain, for example, a competitive or extreme sport, or a focused group activity, such as a debate. As you become absorbed in the activity, you will forget about your stress. If it's just not possible for you to take part in such pursuits, read a gripping thriller, go for a run, or put on headphones and listen to some music you love.

- If you can find some privacy, use a relaxation technique: try progressive relaxation, meditation, or visualization (see page 53), perhaps using a relaxation tape or C.D. Or try a yoga or t'ai chi class (see page 42).

- Just say no: you need to protect your own health and wellbeing.

right > **A full body massage manipulates all your major muscles into a more relaxed state, and is often highly meditative for both the receiver and the massage therapist.**

# wedding stress

The prewedding period can be an especially stressful time. It's completely natural to be apprehensive about practically every aspect of your wedding. In fact, experiencing increased stress shows how much the day means to you and proves you're in touch with your feelings. Don't feel bad or inadequate because you are stressed. The way you manage stress now is crucial to making this a positive time for you and your partner. The planning of a wedding entails innumerable decisions, expenses, expectations, influences, and small details. Most people underestimate the impact this can have, especially the expectation that this will be a perfect time of happiness and fulfilment. A wedding doesn't guarantee that other sources of stress are not out in force—work, moving house, travel, illness, and financial complications only compound prewedding stress. Organizing the honeymoon is a major task in itself. Here's how to cope.

## stress-relieving formulas

- Take your needs seriously: don't overestimate how much you can do all on your own.

- Try to keep your expectations flexible: an event involving so many other people is bound to include the unexpected. If you're very worried about this, keep guest numbers to a minimum.

- Be realistic: especially about your budget.

- Prioritize: don't lose sight of your vision for your wedding and what's most important to you and your partner.

- Cut down on all avoidable sources of stress: if possible, temporarily reduce your working hours. Don't aim to lose an unrealistic amount of weight before the day.

- Keep an eye out for signs that you are beginning to crack.

- Try to stay away from people who make you feel more stressed.

- Don't aim to satisfy everyone: they will all have their own opinions of what you should do. Make sure you don't promise something without thinking it through first.

- Talk to friends and family members who have been through it all before.

- Delegate whatever you can: don't be shy about asking your fiancé, friends, or family to help you with some of the tasks.

- Consider asking someone you trust (implicitly!) to organize the honeymoon for you. This task was traditionally performed by the groom in secret.

- Hire a wedding coordinator or planner to look after many of the details.

- Remember why you're getting married: go out for a romantic meal together if you feel the stress is affecting your relationship. It is totally normal for couples to argue about their wedding!

- Use visualization to guide you through the aspects you are most stressed about: find some quiet time alone, relax, and really visualize the event going smoothly. Repeat several times a day if you need to.

- Talk to people you think might cause problems on the day: ask them to be civil for your sake. But remember that even if other people have disagreements, you'll probably be so caught up in everything else, you won't even notice.

- Make time for fun: equally, have a good cry if you need to.

left > **Shopping for a wedding dress can be a cause of stress, but ultimately should be a treasured moment in the run up to your wedding.**

# relationship difficulties

Almost everyone lists relationship difficulties as being among their main causes of stress. Although we have a need to be connected to others, our relationships are also often the source of our greatest misery. Stress arising from partnerships can develop into problems such as depression, insomnia, and high blood pressure. Understanding this stress—its causes, effects, and the ways that different people respond to it—allows us to make the most of relationships, and survive the inevitable ups and downs. However, most people have to figure it out for themselves. If we are not aware of exactly how we are acting, we may experience relationships as distressing and painful without understanding why.

As common as relationship difficulties are, we often misunderstand them. Much of the time, the causes of the problems stem from hidden patterns within us, not from the behavior or attitudes of others. The problem is we often don't notice the role we play, and many people remain confused about what it takes to create happy, successful, long-term interpersonal relationships. Use the exercise below to explore your patterns of negative behavior, then try to recognize when these patterns are triggered within you, and resist the temptation to act upon them.

## understanding your problem

1 Define your problems, for example, "My husband doesn't pay me enough attention." It might be useful to write them down.

2 Identify the details of the patterns that are causing your relationship problems to begin and continue.

3 Think of ways you might be contributing to the problem, for example by ignoring displays of affection.

4 Take action to disrupt the automatic behavior patterns; you might start to notice small signs of caring, for instance.

5 If the problems continue, keep trying this approach, and then possibly consider relationship counseling (see page 88).

## common negative relationship patterns

### assuming we know how to make a relationship work

Many of us presume our relationships should work automatically because we are good, kind people. We think that if we've found the right partner, or feel strongly in love, it means that the relationship will flourish by itself. We act as if we already know how to make it work. This mistake is encouraged by romantic books and films, but will simply lead to disappointment and stress. Most people don't really know what it takes to have a successful partnership. The truth is often that to succeed in our relationships we must learn to recognize and deal with problems within ourselves and with other people.

### not dealing with anger and criticism

Instead of defending yourself or counter-attacking, assume there may be an element of truth in the accusations or criticisms of others. Benjamin Franklin once said "the sting of any criticism comes from the truth it contains." This also prompts the other person to stop being angry. In discussions, keep the focus only on what you did or didn't do and ignore any generalizations or personal attacks.

below > **In established relationships it is all too easy to allow the everyday to elbow out special moments. It's crucial that you remember to make room for quality time with each other.**

## being critical and blaming

Everyone has the ability to be critical and judgmental of other people. But the tendency to blame someone or something other than ourselves when relationship difficulties occur is very damaging. It prevents us from seeing the part we play and hides the fact that we often have the power to successfully resolve the problems. Constant criticism can lead to arguments and to the putting up of barriers, so try to forgive and take responsibility for your own feelings.

## ignoring other opinions

By immediately rejecting out of hand a partner's opinions and points of view, we risk destroying the relationship. Naturally, we want to be right most of the time, but if we refuse to let others have their say, we risk making them feel hurt and resentful.

## trying to change people

Much relationship stress comes from conscious or unconscious attempts to change or control other people. We try to get others to behave differently, and when they don't change, we become frustrated and angry. If we keep trying to change them and fail, we just get more angry and disappointed, while the other person becomes hostile. Trying to change a partner into someone who thinks, feels, and acts just like us is an act of judgment rather than of respect and appreciation for his or her differences.

## comparing with other relationships

Avoid the tendency to compare yourself to others. Remember that even though other couples may look happier, richer, or more fulfilled on the surface, you never know what really happens behind closed doors.

## how to work toward a successful relationship

- **Make a deep commitment to the relationship: be aware of the loss of freedom that this inevitably involves, and the need to keep your promises in all situations.**

- **Accept the other person exactly as he or she is: with all the faults, weaknesses, and quirks.**

- **Communicate openly and honestly: share your feelings and experiences, and in turn listen attentively.**

- **Take responsibility for your own mistakes and faults.**

- **Be open to negotiation and forgiveness: aim for a good compromise and keep going until you get there.**

- **Use conflict positively: let it stimulate discussion and promote positive changes. Let go of your need always to be right and/or in control.**

- **Make sure you give and receive support, trust, and loyalty.**

- **Have fun together and be friends too!**

right > **The key to maintaining a successful relationship is simple: remember why you liked each other in the first place and continue to have fun together.**

## coping with divorce

The decision to end a relationship sets off a long and challenging process. Even without complicated legal and financial issues, the upheaval is enormous, affecting children, grandparents, friends, and the extended family. The chances are that all family members will experience a substantial drop in their standard of living. So before making the decision, make sure you are certain that there is no alternative, and that you have done all you can to improve matters. Also reflect on the advantages and disadvantages of separating. Think about talking it over with a counselor (see page 88) or getting other expert advice and help (see pages 154–157). A consultation with a legal expert can provide an idea of the likely legal and financial outcomes.

"The process of separation was a kind of loss. But the divorce forced me to rediscover my old self and, with it, some much-needed self-esteem."

Sarah, publisher

## how to survive

Separation and divorce are two of the most painful life events you could have to face. They can lead you to question everything in life, even your own identity and your ability to cope by yourself. Divorce highlights your fears and sensitivities. Old wounds from the past might resurface. You will need to recover your self-esteem, which will surely take time. The stress of divorce can feel overwhelming for most people, so use every management strategy from Chapter 2 to help you cope with the pressure (see page 38).

## ways to care for yourself and others

- Consider joining a support group and going through mediation: it can lead to better communication and less confrontation with your ex-partner.

- Rather than withdrawing socially, surround yourself with friends: remember how important they are in providing support, perspective, and practical help.

- Learn how to balance giving and receiving: you do not have to be perfect.

- Don't beat yourself up over what you should have done: stop the self-criticism, guilt, and negative self-talk. You can't change the past, so try to learn the lessons and then focus on a positive future.

- Set aside time just for yourself: you need this to help you find balance.

left > **Remember to find time for yourself in the midst of what can be a maelstrom of activity that surrounds life events such as divorce.**

- Don't worry about what other people might be thinking.

- Have a clear-out: decluttering helps to simplify your environment and can also be very liberating emotionally.

- Focus on what really needs to be done and prioritize: then break up the tasks into smaller steps that can be completed in a short space of time.

- You might have to begin work after a long break: look for a manageable job, or get training in a marketable skill. Bringing home your own money is satisfying and creates independence. It also sets a positive example for children.

- Work toward forgiveness and moving on: don't deny your anger, but don't let it drain your energy by getting stuck in resentment.

- Don't be scared of going out on your own: open up to new people.

## money worries

In the middle of the difficulties of ending a relationship, you may also have to deal with financial affairs. This can be particularly tricky if there is an atmosphere of mistrust because of the breakup. Many divorces are actually caused by money issues. The cost of the divorce depends on many factors, including income, mortgage or loans, the length of the marriage, and whether you have children. Most couples agree on a financial settlement rather than going to court, but even so, a typical divorce settlement can take over a year to finalize. Deciding on child-maintenance payments can be especially fraught.

### financial destressing skills

- **Make it a priority to learn how to budget and manage your finances: especially if your ex-partner used to deal with most of the financial matters.**

- **Get advice on how your pension, savings, and investments might be affected by divorce (see pages 154–157).**

- **Close joint accounts as soon as possible.**

- **List all your assets and debts.**

- **Seek advice on the financial decisions you need to make: most important if you are selling a home. Ask for help from your legal team or an organization that supports those going through a divorce (see pages 154–157).**

left > **Children can suffer when a relationship breaks down, but by talking to them and encouraging them to have fun, you can ease this painful process.**

# children and stress

While most adapt well, some children going through divorce will suffer significant adjustment problems. They will, at the least, be anxious about their relationships within the family and about the disruption in their lives. Much depends on how you handle it—you can make an enormous difference in how well they cope. Look for signs of distress, such as increased clingy behavior, tantrums, fear of separation, anxiety at bedtime, changes in eating and sleeping patterns, thumb-sucking, bed-wetting, headaches or stomach aches, increased aggression or perfectionism. If you observe these symptoms, let children know you understand they are upset and that it's OK to talk about it to you or someone else. Help them express themselves in whichever way they can, and seek help from your doctor or a counselor (see page 88) if signs of distress continue.

## ways to reduce stress on children

- Give them as much reassurance as possible: above all, tell them they are not responsible for the breakup.

- Talk over what is happening in a way they can comprehend.

- Be open to their questions: encourage children to talk about their feelings, but don't force them to talk.

- Encourage children to maintain their relationship with the other parent.

- Don't criticize the other parent: nor demand exclusive loyalty, or use children to hurt your ex-partner.

- Avoid looking to your children for support or guidance.

- Maintain normal domestic routines as far as you possibly can.

# coping during holidays

For children from divorced or separated families, holidays and vacations can be difficult. If you focus on the needs of the children, use a good support system, and take care of yourself both emotionally and physically, holidays can be happy and fulfilling regardless of the family structure.

## how to reduce conflict

- Be aware that holidays are always tricky and magnify existing problems.

- For younger children: don't make them decide which parent to spend the holiday with—this causes enormous distress.

- Keep all of your expectations realistic: especially those expectations that you have about yourself.

- Don't try to outdo each other: don't compensate or make up for problems or lack of time with expensive gifts or other indulgences.

# stress at work

Work is a major source of tension. Stress can make a potentially enjoyable job miserable, and your work can make you ill. Studies show that the majority of days taken off work are caused by stress. In small doses, workplace stress can improve your performance, but if it is sustained and outside your control, it can have extremely negative effects on your health and wellbeing. Stress at work can originate from the demands of the job and its environment, your boss or colleagues, working hours, job insecurity, and pay (or lack of it!). Developments in communications technology—cellphones, email, video conferencing—and the move to short-term contracts, outsourcing, and home working has drastically changed the nature of the work that many of us do, causing even more stress.

## symptoms of work stress

- **Loss of concentration**

- **Anxiety and/or depression**

- **Difficulty sleeping**

- **Anger and aggression**

- **Conflict at home**

- **Drinking or smoking more**

- **High blood pressure, headaches, or stomach disorders**

below and right >

Work-related stress does not have to be overwhelming. Simple tactics such as a foot roller under the desk or exercising with colleagues in the lunch hour can alleviate many of the symptoms.

## the pressure of increased demands

Modern workplaces are going through intense changes—reorganizations, takeovers, mergers, and diversifications. The pressure for a company to survive filters down to increased demands on employees. Unrealistic expectations to meet high performance targets, introduce new technology, and increase hours can lead to unreasonable stress as employees are expected constantly to adapt  and learn new skills. The workplace culture may also alter, for example, by moving premises, adopting new methods of communication, and introducing different styles of leadership. Then there's the stress of office politics, direct bullying, or harassment. For all these reasons, you should monitor your stress levels and actively look for solutions when they start rising.

## how to ease stress at work

- Anticipate: be prepared for occasional changes, but don't expect to be able to adapt straightaway.

- Protect and value your time off: don't be pressured into working longer hours than you want to.

- Keep up the positive coping strategies: exercise, relaxation, and good nutrition help.

- Try to get on with colleagues: but keep some emotional distance.

- If you are being bullied or harassed, keep a record of the situation: then approach someone trustworthy to help.

- Build up three months' salary in savings: just in case your job comes to an abrupt end.

- Use stress-busting strategies (see page 38): work especially on goal setting and good time management.

- Be aware of your behavior patterns: hard-working, driven people with high standards are at higher risk of the negative effects of stress. If this sounds like you, pay serious attention to any symptoms.

- Learn to say no: if your workload is high, limit your additional commitments or responsibilities. Delegate tasks to others as much as possible.

## repetitive strain injury and back problems

Repeating the same task every day damages tendons, nerves, and muscles, an ailment known as repetitive strain injury (R.S.I.). The damage can be triggered by computer work, accumulating slowly. Certain typing techniques and body positions increase the risk by putting strain on tendons and nerves in hands, wrists, arms, shoulders, neck, and back. Symptoms include pain, stiffness, soreness, burning, tingling, coldness, numbness, or lack of strength in the hands, wrists, fingers, fore-arms, or elbows. Back injury at work affects four out of five people at some stage in life.

### how to prevent injury

- Have a specialist check your working posture at your desk.
- Take regular breaks.
- Vary your actions, for example, swap which hand controls the mouse.
- To avoid back pain, use an upright chair and keep your back straight. Be sure your feet are flat to the floor, or use a footrest.
- Regularly get up and walk around.

## coping with job loss

Losing a job can lead to many stresses—about loss of confidence and a social network as well as of income and security. It's reasonable to have initial feelings of anger and uncertainty. The next step is to take action. Have faith in yourself and look to the next challenge. Try to keep up your energy levels and confidence. Now is the time to decide what you want to do in your future career, so take a step back and gather your thoughts. Consider your resources and transferable skills, and talk things over with someone supportive. So many people are laid off these days that there is no longer a stigma attached. Job loss brings up stressful financial considerations. Plan wisely and take advice—if you have a lump sum, you might be advised to pay off debts and invest, for example.

right > **The process of adjustment needed when retiring from work can be taxing. But don't forget that this is also a golden opportunity to enjoy activities that were previously crammed into tight weekends.**

## the challenge of retirement

Finishing work can be a difficult transition. You can lose your social network as well as your role as worker and provider. In some people this may trigger mild depression and a sense of emptiness. It can also be a challenging time for a partner, who has to adapt to having someone else around the home all day. This can lead to irritation and frustration.

Working is a key source of satisfaction and connection to society. Without work, you must look for these essentials elsewhere. Plan what to do in your retirement before you get there. Look for a sense of purpose in the new opportunities that arise, using all that extra spare time to pursue a hobby or activity that has always intrigued you, or to travel or study.

# changing job

Feeling unsatisfied in your job can be a subtle, but constant, source of stress. Although changing to a new job, or an entirely new career, can be a daunting thought, see it as a positive movement toward reducing stress and becoming more fulfilled.

## making a fresh start

Have you lost interest in your current career, or were you never very interested in the first place? Have you been made redundant, or feel your talents and creativity are being wasted? If so, you might be thinking about a change of direction. Many people long to change their career, but are put off by fear of the unknown. It is a scary thought—in a new profession, you will not be able to rely on the skills and knowledge you have now. You might have to compete with younger or more experienced people, and it might lead to a drop in income. There are undoubtedly risks involved, but stay positive: many of your experiences and abilities will be transferable, and a fresh start is an opportunity to set out new goals, or pursue dreams you have kept hidden for years. Use the stress-relieving formulas set out opposite to put you in the right frame of mind.

## reducing the risks of career moves

- List your likes and dislikes, strengths and weaknesses: think about which types of jobs fit your preferences and have a brainstorm with your partner or a friend.

- Specify the elements of your current job that you do and don't like: maybe you could find ways to give your current job an overhaul so it fits your requirements. If not, decide which aspects of a new direction appeal to you and why. Make sure a new job will definitely include those elements, by thoroughly researching it.

- Plan a career move while still in paid employment: this takes extra effort and may be what prevents many people from making the change.

- Be really sure of every detail: perhaps visit a careers advisor or life coach to discuss all the options.

left > **Job interviews can be daunting, but a change in career can be one of the most liberating and exciting experiences you will enjoy in your professional life.**

- Research your new direction: find out what kind of training you need and where to get work experience. Consider whether you can train while working in your current job, and, if not, whether you can afford to stop working while you train.

- Talk to people in the position you seek: they are often more than happy to give advice. Build up these contacts for the future—they could help you find a vacancy.

- If you decide to be your own boss: get advice on setting up your own company, tax, pension and salary issues, and on employing other people.

- Don't be disheartened if your aim seems a long way off: remind yourself why you want to get there, and remember how unsatisfied you currently feel.

- Keep your goals realistic: don't risk setting yourself up for a big disappointment.

- Plan carefully: this dramatically reduces the risks and stress involved in a career change.

"Retraining was a big leap in the dark, but my new career has made me glad to go to work each morning."

**Celine, massage therapist**

# beginning a new job

Firstly, be sure that changing job is really the solution to your problems—many people find themselves feeling just as bored and restless once settled into a new role. When the exciting honeymoon period is over, the stresses might prove fairly similar to those you had before. Still, for some, a change is as good as a rest. When you begin a new role there are many fresh skills to learn and new people to meet. The environment can be equally unknown and daunting. A new job marks the beginning of a new era in your life, too, one in which you have to prove yourself and be accepted. This can become quite stressful, but is positive rather than negative stress.

## stress-reducing tips

- Prepare well: do some research on the company so that you aren't going into the complete unknown.

- Plan ahead for your first day: have everything prepared and ready the night before and map your journey so you don't arrive flustered.

- Check what you need to bring with you: bank details, references, equipment.

- Don't be late: leave with plenty of time.

- Hide your fear: you are bound to be a bit nervous, but try not to make it too obvious—first impressions often count. Remember that everyone in your workplace was new once, too.

- Be enthusiastic: show initiative so you are noticed, appreciated, and given responsibility.

- Be good: in your first few days, don't receive or send personal emails or make phone calls, nor ask too many questions about holidays!

- Get involved: be friendly and willing. Try to remember names, at least those of people you work closely with.

- Observe your colleagues: look for clues on dress code and manner of interaction. Take notes on any information you are given.

- Don't struggle: if you are unsure about anything, ask (intelligent) questions.

- Don't be too quick to complain or argue: give things a chance first.

- Ease up the pressure: remember that you are only human and unlikely to get everything right first time.

right > **Meditating at home the night before can help you enjoy your first day in a new job.**

## relieving nerves the night before

• Get everything you can ready, so you know you will be fully prepared in the morning.

• Aim for a good night's sleep—don't stay out late with friends the night before.

• Have a long warm bath to help you wind down before bedtime.

• Call friends and family for support, but avoid talking to anxious people.

• Try a relaxation technique (see page 48).

• Recall your past successes to build up feelings of confidence.

# becoming a parent

If you're considering trying for a baby there are many actions you can take to keep the stress to a minimum before, during, and after pregnancy.

## making the decision

Seeing your newborn baby must be one of the greatest joys in life. The decision to have a baby cannot be taken lightly, but the rewards are enormous. It will completely change your life, and so needs careful planning. You need to provide a secure environment in which children can grow up happy and content. Think about whether you and your partner are emotionally and financially able to support a family, and whether you have friends or an extended family to lean on. Use the following thoughts to think through these stressful practicalities. Once done, you can immerse yourself in the fun side of becoming a parent—deciding on a name, decorating a beautiful nursery, and buying tiny clothes.

### financial strain

In the first year of life, a baby will set you back an average of two to three months' salary. You might also need a bigger car or home, and want to plan for the cost of education and the increased expense of vacations. For those without savings or a reasonable income, all these issues could present a big financial challenge—assess your savings and look into statutory benefits and maternity/paternity leave entitlements to reduce your stress load.

### day-to-day changes

Think about who will care for the child day-to-day—will one of you stay at home full-time; will you look for a nanny or daycare? Aim for a solution that best fits everyone's needs.

left > **Becoming a parent for the first time can be daunting, but by looking after yourself and your baby many of the stress factors can be alleviated.**

## becoming a mom

Motherhood is both exciting and scary. There is so much you can worry about—the sacrifice of your easy, adult-pleasing lifestyle, loss of earnings and time for yourself, a complete revolution in the relationship with your partner. But this is a particularly bad time to be stressed for your and your baby's health. Pregnancy can be an extremely emotional experience, especially difficult if you don't feel you're getting enough support. Make sure you have friends, family, and professionals on hand that you feel able to talk to.

If you are planning to be a working mom, be prepared for the effects motherhood will have. Breaking the news of your pregnancy at work could be stressful, especially if you have a difficult boss. Know your rights, and ask about flexible working, or perhaps reducing hours.

### stress-relieving tips

- **Once you have decided to go ahead, give your baby the best start in life by taking care of yourself.**

- **Keep on top of stress using the strategies in Chapter 2 (see page 38).**

- **Visit your doctor to start prenatal checkups as soon as you can.**

- **Eat well and get enough exercise.**

- **Stop drinking alcohol and smoking.**

- **Take a pregnancy multivitamin supplement that includes folic acid.**

## surviving the birth

This could prove to be one of the most stressful days of your life! Writing a birth plan weeks before the event will help make sure you have thought about all eventualities. Consider where the birth will take place, whether the father and/or a supportive friend or relative will be there, the type of birth you hope for, and what kinds of interventions you want (and don't want). Of course it could all change on the day, but at least you'll have reduced your stress by considering all the options open to you.

Home births tend to lead to fewer medical problems, but if it would worry you to not be in hospital, then go with your instincts. Visit the labor ward or birthing center beforehand, so it's not completely new. Learn stress-relieving breathing techniques at antenatal classes. Plan your journey to the hospital and have your bag packed and ready by the front door.

"Becoming a dad for the first time is every bit as thrilling as people tell you. And, believe me, every bit exhausting!"
**Barry, new father**

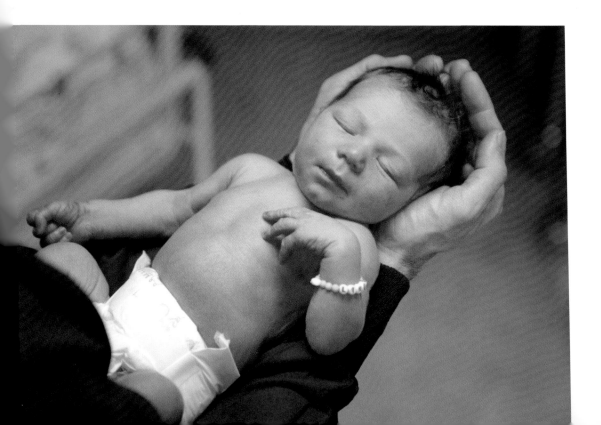

## stress-reduction tactics for labor

- **Give yourself numerous options for finding the best position: ask for extra pillows, a birthing ball, or birthing chair.**

- **Consider water birth: think about it before the event.**

- **Have someone hold your hand: try firm massage pressure on the lower back, perhaps with a jasmine oil blend (see pages 54–57) reputed to speed labor and relieve pain.**

- **Play music: helps distract you and rhythmic dancing can help to strengthen contractions.**

- **Use a T.E.N.S. machine for pain relief: get familiar with it before the day.**

- **Ask questions: as many as you want, and even the embarrassing ones!**

- **Don't be perfect: get all the help you might need.**

## becoming a dad

You may experience a wide range of emotions when you learn you are going to be a father. It can be as worrying a time for you as it is for your partner. You will have many questions: find answers from friends and relatives, books and the internet. Try to get to antenatal classes, too, where all aspects of becoming a parent are discussed and you can find more practical advice. Your support at this time is crucial in keeping your partner's stress levels down, so give reassurance when she needs it.

If you have decided together that your partner is going to stop working or reduce her hours, you might be concerned about the pressure of being the main breadwinner of the household. Keep the dialogue open with your partner and voice your fears, either to her or someone else you can trust.

Be prepared for the time around the birth to be exhausting and physically draining for you as well as for your partner. Consider ways that you can manage your own stress. Look into your rights and find out about paternity leave from work. Think also about taking annual leave around the time of the birth—many men wish they had been around more at this time to support their partners and bond with the new baby.

While at home during the first few days and weeks of parenthood, you will take on the brunt of dealing with friends and family. It is likely that your partner will be consumed with the abrupt reality of motherhood: breastfeeding, sleepless nights, nappy changing, and her own physical exhaustion. Be prepared to gently field calls and monitor how tired your partner is becoming when receiving visits or making them. This is your first experience of being the family protector!

left > **To relieve the anxieties of first-time fatherhood, it is crucial that you make every effort to bond with your new baby.**

# stressful families

Stress caused by those close to you is hard to escape. Parenting and visiting relatives are potential minefields of pressure and anxiety. As they say, "You can choose your friends, but you can't choose your family."

## the stress of parenting

Children bring happiness and fun, but also tiredness and stress. Your daily routine changes, your sleep is disturbed, and new pressures arise. Whether you stay at home or work, are single or married, have one child or six, the challenges are enormous. Remaining calm and collected all the time is an impossible goal. When the small hassles add up, building the pressure until you are ready to burst, try some of the coping strategies below.

### ways to reduce the strain

- Remember it's not meant to be easy: any problems you have will have been coped with by many parents before.

- Adjust your priorities: previous standards of order and neatness might have to change. Don't take on unnecessary duties and responsibilities while kids are young.

- Don't feel guilty: every parent gets stressed and is sometimes overwhelmed. If you're doing your best, absolve yourself of guilt (easier said than done!).

- Accept any help offered: if you can afford it, pay someone to help with cleaning, shopping, or laundry, especially at busy times.

- Take advice: from people whose opinion you trust, and from experts when issues arise.

- Share the responsibility: make sure your partner is doing their fair share.

- Safeguard important affairs: set up a lockable filing system for important documents, and use it.

- Look after yourself: use every stress-management skill going (see page 40) and be alert to symptoms.

- Take time to relax: this sets a great example for your children.

- Prepare for the next day and give yourself extra time to get ready before going out.

- Anticipate: try to predict and prepare for problems before they arise.

- Write lists and use a calendar: you can't be expected to remember everything.

- Keep communicating with your children: take time out of your busy routine to spend on easing their worries.

# balancing work and home life

Working and bringing up children is tricky and often challenging. In times of stress you may feel as if your work and home lives are both suffering from lack of time and attention. Decide on your priorities in both spheres, but try to stay flexible. During the tough times, remember and focus on why you made these choices.

## how to diffuse the conflict

- **Build up resources: support networks, emergency funds, and your own energy.**

- **Use effective coping strategies.**

- **Be realistic: don't put impossible pressure on yourself and your partner.**

- **Plan ahead: get help when you need it, and look for creative solutions.**

above > **Your ability to relax will have a direct impact on how your children deal with stress in later life. Relaxing together teaches them important lessons—as well as being an opportunity to enjoy each other's company.**

# single parenting

Everyone finds parenting hard at times, but single parenting has added pressures. One of the most difficult aspects of single parenting is not having another adult in the house to offer support and validation. Working outside the home can give you a sense of purpose, but feeling that you have to cope with too much will pile on the stress. This stress can in turn affect the way you relate to your children. There's nearly always something you can do to reduce the stress you feel and make life easier, and there are often people who are willing to help.

## destressing tips

above > **Being a single parent is one of life's biggest challenges. But your ability to play with your child will help to create a good atmosphere between the two of you, so that you become each other's support system.**

• Develop and nurture several sources of support: perhaps team up with other parents—it's always easier to cope if you have people to turn to.

• Get on top of your finances. Know your budget and get advice if necessary.

• Reassure your children: let them know how much you love them and how much you value them.

• Beginning a new relationship: explain what is happening, but don't introduce new partners to your kids too soon.

• Fit in time for yourself: use this time to explore your feelings. Be kind to yourself and build up your confidence if it has been damaged.

## stress from relatives

Many people feel guilty if they don't enjoy spending time with relatives, but don't worry, it doesn't make you a bad person, just an honest one (best not tell them though!). Look for the good in others and try to see circumstances from their point of view, at least temporarily.

### destressing visits to relatives

- Keep expectations realistic: if you predict unpleasantness, don't plan to stay for too long. Take a deep breath and remember it'll be over soon!

- Be prepared: if you anticipate some criticism and stress-inducing questions, have a stock of (reasonable) responses ready-prepared.

- Strike a bargain with children: perhaps they should receive a small reward for being well behaved all day.

- If you get upset: go for a walk, take a nap, or find somewhere private to call a friend and get it off your chest.

- Pack a good book that lifts your spirits.

### destressing visits from relatives

- Plan in advance: where they will sleep, what kind of food you will feed them, and how you can budget effectively to meet extra costs.

- Let them help: accept offers of help with the cooking, washing up, and anything else that comes up.

- Don't attempt an impressive or elaborate meal: stock up the fridge and freezer with food that's quick and simple to prepare.

- Don't fuel tension: if arguments are likely to arise, don't provide your guests with too much alcohol.

- When you go out, don't feel obliged to cover all the expenses.

- Play games together: to create an atmosphere of fun.

- Resist pressure: there is no need to fill up every minute with activities.

# moving home

Moving can seem a very daunting task. Although it's usually a positive event, it sits up there with the biggest life stressors. Not only is there the packing to worry about, but the legal and financial implications, and if you have to transfer your children to a new school, the event can begin to feel like organized chaos. The best advice to minimize stress is to plan everything well in advance, using the check lists on these pages.

## stress busting a few weeks ahead

- Get quotes from removal companies: use one that comes with a friend's recommendation if possible.

- If moving yourself: start gathering strong boxes and stock up on parcel tape and marker pens. Save newspapers for wrapping breakables, and ask around for sturdy storage crates and bubble wrap.

- Enlist help for the day: to help carry and load, and to clean the emptied house.

- Measure up: ensure large items of furniture fit the new house or organize someone to remove glass from a window if necessary.

- Make an itinerary: room by room list all the items to be moved, stating exactly where each one is going.

- Start packing as early as possible: makes it easier to jettison unnecessary junk. Anything that hasn't been used since your last move can probably go.

- Call the refuse service: find out which bulky objects they will collect to save time disposing of large items.

- Label boxes on the top and sides: mark the fragile ones and know which contain important documents. Don't make boxes too heavy to lift.

- Inform utility and service companies: as soon as possible let electricity, gas, and telephone suppliers know your moving date and arrange also to be connected at the new place. Never expect this part of the move to go without a hitch!

- Set up a redirection service for mail: list all companies who need to know your new details, including home, car, life insurance, and pensions.

- Make up a change of address card: tell friends and family your new address and phone number.

- Arrange a babysitter: young children and moving don't mix well. Also plan what to do with pets.

- Make a survival kit: everything you'll need for the first night after the move—food and utensils, toiletries, nightclothes, bottled water, toolkit, and flashlight.

## stress busting on the day

above > In the midst of frenetic activity, try not to forget that moving house is the start of an exciting new journey.

- Empty the refrigerator.

- Do a final check of every room: don't forget the garage, garden shed, and loft.

- Pack a box of essentials for moving day: coffee, tea bags, clean mugs, spoons, sugar, biscuits, towels, toilet paper, garbage bags, and scissors.

- Make a leaving checklist: are windows closed, doors locked, light sockets and electrical switches turned off, especially those for boilers and heating?

# vacation stress

Vacations are intended to be relaxing and carefree, but the stresses new places and unbroken time with family sometimes bring can leave you yearning to get back to the workplace. High hopes can bring disappointment when the unexpected happens. Mistakes are made and maps read wrongly, illness can strike at any time, and good weather can rarely be guaranteed.

## ways to ease the pressure:

### stress-relieving formulas

• Try to take longer vacations: short breaks can be exciting, but leave little time to unwind. You will feel more relaxed after two weeks' away than one.

• Use all your annual vacation allowance: it is essential to your wellbeing, and by changing your perspective can make you more efficient at work.

• Budget well: establish an amount in advance and keep to it to resist the stress of the payback months later.

• Make lists: work out what you need to take and gather everything together in advance.

• Don't aim to do too much in a short space of time: remember the importance of lying on the beach or by the pool, reading, taking time over food, and just doing nothing.

• Anticipate disruptions: check whether the hotel is in a quiet or "lively" area, and make sure flight times will not leave you recovering for days afterward.

• Confirm the details of your travel insurance.

• Make hand luggage work: include absolute essentials, including a small first-aid kit and important phone numbers.

• Photocopy credit cards, passports, flight tickets, hotel details and insurance: keep them separate from the originals.

• Protect and survive: use sunblock and avoid the midday sun; don't waste valuable days nursing hangovers!

• Find out about immunizations well in advance.

• If taking part in dangerous sports, check the qualifications of the instructor.

• Take a range of distractions for children: avoid those that make too much mess, such as paint and modeling clay.

• Keep everyone happy: bear in mind every person's needs and stay open to negotiation before you go and after you arrive.

## leaving work behind

Many people have trouble switching off and relaxing and they can even start to feel bored on vacation. If you're not used to having much free time it can be hard to leave behind the buzz and activity that work brings.

### tips to distance you from work

- **Leave your cellphone at home: avoid the temptation to check your emails if the hotel has an internet connection and maybe even think about taking your watch off for the duration of the holiday.**

- **Anticipate work-related problems: before leaving the workplace, try to predict issues that might arise and leave instructions for others to deal with them.**

- **Clear your desk: returning to a clean slate prevents a little of that sinking feeling that accompanies your return.**

- **Don't aim to get too much done in the few days before and after your vacation.**

- **On vacation write down work-related thoughts as they pop up: then empty your mind of that source of stress.**

"A good vacation is over when you begin to yearn for your work."

Morris Fishbein

# managing money

Woody Allen said, "Money is better than poverty, if only for financial reasons." Nevertheless, money brings with it a great deal of stress for nearly everyone. The panic some of us feel about money issues can prevent us from addressing the problem and lead to financial affairs getting worse. Debt and the difficulties of balancing a budget affect most people these days. The cost of being a student, buying a home, and myriad everyday expenses—plus the ease of getting a loan—can add up to a big headache. It is possible to remove the fear and mystery of money matters and get on top of the situation. These questionnaires and positive strategies will help you make a start.

## assessing your financial affairs

To start you thinking in the right way about your finances, spend a few minutes jotting down answers to the following questions:

1 How much money do you have in savings and investments?

2 How much money do you owe, including student loans and mortgage?

3 Are you only paying off the minimum charge on your debts each month?

4 Do you know exactly what direct debits and other automatic payments you are making?

5 What is the minimum amount you need to live on each month?

6 How much of your income is left for paying off debts or for saving?

7 What do you need to save for (wedding, vacation, etc)?

8 How much do you spend on unnecessary items every day? If you're not sure where your money goes, keep a spending diary for a week or a month—you may be surprised.

### analyzing your answers

Do your responses highlight problems or reveal a pattern of affairs you would like to change? Let them help you focus attention on areas that could improve. When you have spent some time pondering, use the table opposite to have a go at coming up with possible solutions. A sample has been filled in to start you thinking in the right direction.

# my financial problems and potential solutions

| money-related problem | possible solution | action to take |
|---|---|---|
| Daily spending too high. | Stop buying expensive food during the day. | Buy sandwich ingredients and cheaper snacks at the supermarket. |
| | | |
| | | |
| | | |
| | | |
| | | |

## taking control

Don't ignore financial problems; they won't just go away! Be brave and open all bank and store-card statements. Attempt to break the impulse-buying habit—try giving yourself a spending allowance or pay with cash to make you think twice. Remember you'll appreciate things all the more if you save up for them. However, money management isn't all about spending less—think about whether you are getting the salary you deserve. Consider asking for a rise, or think about other ways you could increase your income.

# dealing with debt

Uncontrolled debts are a worry, no matter how hard you try not to think about them. Decide that you are going to face them head-on and take action sooner rather than later. Some of the following strategies may help:

## stress-busting formulas

- **List your debts: add in the amount of interest you are being charged on each (be brave, this could get depressing).**

- **Prioritize paying off those debts with the highest interest rates: move all the money you can to a 0% interest credit card, but be aware that this rate probably won't last forever.**

- **Destroy some cards: keep one or two credit cards but cut up the rest.**

- **Be more frugal: cut out luxuries and beware of the lure of internet shopping.**

- **Set realistic goals: how much can you afford to pay off and how much can you save?**

- **Add to your income: think about increasing your hours at work, selling some valuables, or renting out the spare room.**

- **Seek expert help: take advantage of expert help and free advice available (see pages 154–157).**

## understanding your credit rating

There are a number of reasons why you might be turned down for credit. Your credit rating might be affected, for example, if you have had problems paying utility or credit card bills in the past. You can find out what details are held about your credit history by contacting a credit reference agency. Ask for a copy of your personal credit file (it can also be ordered online). If the information on your file is incorrect, you can add a "statement of correction" of about 200 words, which will be given to lenders in the future. Improve your credit rating by making sure you are on the electoral register, paying utility and credit card bills on time, and not making a series of applications for loans in the hope of finding someone who will lend you money.

## saving and investments

When you have paid off debts, it is important to build up savings. Ideally, you should put aside three months' income in an easily accessible account. A good way to save is to set up a monthly standing order. Aim to save 10 percent of your income. Look around for a savings account or in the U.K. an I.S.A. (tax-free individual savings account) with a good rate of interest. According to the American money expert Alvin Hall, the key to successful investing is to choose a company that has good growth potential, and a strong market position. He also recommends investing no more money than you can afford to lose.

It's never too early to start thinking about your pension. The earlier you start putting money toward it, the more comfortable your retirement will be. Get some good advice and start paying into a scheme as soon as possible. It's the only way to stop your parents nagging!

above > **The economics of cooking with cheap, fresh ingredients rather than heating up expensive ready meals may introduce you to an unexpected upside to debt management: a healthier diet.**

# coping with bereavement

The death of someone close to us is the most severe stressor we will ever face. Bereavement brings a high risk of mental and physical health problems for a long time afterward. Although it is a completely natural process, grieving can be profoundly painful and distressing. It causes deep sadness and usually those who are grieving become withdrawn. Everyone takes a different length of time to go though the different stages. As well as the suffering the loss of a loved one brings, death can evoke uncomfortable thoughts about our own mortality. Those around us might not be willing or capable of discussing these fears. The death of a spouse in particular can have serious physical, mental, behavioral, and emotional consequences.

## common reactions to bereavement

Grief symptoms can last months or years. The reactions you might have will depend on your personality and the circumstances of the loss. Any existing emotional problems are likely to be heightened. It's possible to experience any reaction normally related to stress, including some or all of the following:

### emotional reactions
Shock, numbness, sadness, longing, irritability, anger, guilt, anxiety, loneliness, fatigue, and helplessness.

### common thought patterns
Disbelief, confusion, difficulty in concentrating, being preoccupied, even thinking you see or hear the deceased person.

### physical reactions
Headaches, tightness in the throat or chest, nausea, weakness, lowered immunity to infections.

### behavioral reactions
Problems sleeping, loss of appetite, crying, avoiding others, restlessness, and nightmares.

### emotional reactions
Extremely common and more likely if grief is repressed or if the ability to adapt to the loss is delayed, for example, if it occurs immediately before another major life event.

# surviving the stages of grief

Grieving is a very personal experience, and no one can tell anyone else how to grieve. However, people usually go through all the stages detailed before they adapt to the loss. Learning about these stages can be reassuring: it shows that what you are experiencing is normal. The stages may occur in a different order or overlap, and vary in the amount of time they occupy.

## stage 1. denial and shock
In this stage people refuse to believe the death has occurred and try to believe that life hasn't changed. This is a natural coping mechanism, but can be very disturbing for yourself and others. To move on, you have to face reality and begin accepting support.

## stage 2. anger and guilt
You may blame others for the loss, or become angry with yourself. Experts agree that it's much better to express this anger than to keep it in, which could lead to depression or other long-lasting and negative consequences.

## getting help

**If you find your grief is overwhelming you and starting to affect your relationships, look for professional support (see pages 88-91). Although it's impossible to reduce the significance of the loss, by getting the right kind of help to face the pain and meet the challenge of new circumstances, you will be taking an important step toward feeling better. The more support you get in interpreting your feelings, the easier they are to accept. Talking it through can help you see events and their meanings clearly.**

## stage 3. anxiety
This can range from a slight sense of insecurity to a strong panic attack. The source of the anxiety may be fear that you won't be able to look after yourself on your own, that you'll never recover, and a heightened sense of your own mortality.

## stage 4. bargaining
With yourself or with God. Many people believe there is something they or someone else can do to change reality.

## stage 5. deep sadness and despair
This is inevitable for all who experience a significant loss and can be the hardest and longest-lasting stage of grief, with the most physical symptoms. Now is time to work through painful memories and start coping with the changes that result from the loss.

## stage 6. acceptance
The final stage. Sadness is less intense and you come to accept that life goes on. Energy returns and you begin to look to the future.

right > **The loss of a loved one can plunge you into unexpected solitude. Time alone during the grieving process can be a comfort, but if it isn't, never hesitate to ask for help.**

## withstanding society's pressures

Western society is not comfortable with open displays of distress, and encourages grief to be hidden away. These limits are not psychologically healthy, nor helpful to people struggling to adapt to loss. Being aware of these pressures can help those who are grieving to understand they are not overreacting, and that they need an outlet in which openly to show their grief.

## supporting others through bereavement

Expressions of grief can be painful to observe in those you care about. This pain prevents people from getting closely involved. But if you feel you can give support and are prepared to do so, offer to share some of your time.

Grief symptoms (see page 140) can sometimes seem strange or alarming. Read about the responses and treat the person going through them with calm reassurance and understanding.

If the bereaved person was a caregiver for their loved one in the days before the death,

he or she may already have developed anxiety or depression, which might be compounded with guilt about feeling relief or a lack of emotional response (some people work through a loss in advance).

Watch for signs that the bereaved needs more help than he or she is receiving. If he or she talks about suicide, relies heavily on drugs or alcohol, or is not beginning to recover after a year or more, think about suggesting counseling (see page 88), or visiting a doctor to discuss antidepressants and other help.

# dealing with anxiety and depression

When stress builds up, and we don't manage it effectively, it has the potential to develop into longer term problems. Anxiety and depression are the most common mental disorders arising from severe stress. They can often be present at the same time, in which case, they tend to make each other worse.

## understanding anxiety

Anxiety is a fear that something bad is going to happen. This becomes a long-term problem when that anxiety is not based on a specific event but is an ongoing worry. The pattern can be learned in childhood from anxious parents. Experiencing some anxiety in the face of stress is natural; it is not natural when it is a constant feature of life. For people experiencing anxiety, as soon as one worry is overcome, another will immediately replace it. Good stress management (see page 38) can prevent such everyday hassles from sustaining a state of constant anxiety.

### types of anxiety problem

These problems act to increase the stress in life, and, in so doing, can set up a vicious circle. They are usually treated with counseling (see page 88), possibly combined with medication, so don't delay in getting help from a doctor. If anxiety is "pushed down" it can manifest in a wide range of physical symptoms. Some of the more likely problems are headaches, high blood pressure or palpitations, an upset stomach, and muscle pain. In the modern world, sadly, these problems are widespread.

### generalized anxiety

Ongoing anxiety, worry, and concern with no obvious triggers. This is the most common form of anxiety and can result in poor concentration, a feeling of being on edge or easily startled, dizziness, fatigue, and trouble sleeping. It is often reduced by exercise, relaxation, and the other stress-management strategies explored in Chapter 2 (see page 38).

### panic attacks

Short bouts of extreme, overwhelming fear. You might feel as if you are dying, about to have a heart attack, or can't breathe. Panic attacks are rarely dangerous.

### obsessive-compulsive disorder

Involves persistent thoughts and the strong need to carry out certain actions, such as checking that objects are in the right place. These fixations can occupy many hours a day.

"Anxiety is the handmaiden of creativity."

T.S. Eliot

### posttraumatic stress disorder

Develops in response to an intensely stressful event, usually a form of threat to life. It involves frequent intrusive thoughts going back to the traumatic event, and can last indefinitely if not worked through.

### phobias

Arise when fear linked to something specific becomes so strong that it is out of proportion to its original cause. Some phobias, such as agoraphobia (fear of open spaces) can seriously interfere with everyday life.

above > **Recognizing your own anxiety patterns and what works best to alleviate them is all part of responsible management of stress levels. Many people return to their massage therapist at times of acute stress.**

# understanding depression

Clinical depression is far more common than we would like to believe, and it is increasing. Anyone can develop it—between 5 and 10 percent of the population are suffering from the illness to some extent at any one time. Depression involves much more than ordinary sadness. Understanding more about it can help you get better—don't allow yourself to believe that you'll never beat it.

## common symptoms

**Depression can include any or all of these symptoms, and they last for weeks or months:**

- **Loss of interest and enjoyment in life**

- **Hopelessness**

- **Loss of motivation**

- **Feelings of inadequacy**

- **Irritability**

- **Changes in eating behavior**

- **Insomnia**

- **Fatigue**

- **Thinking about suicide: if you feel this way, talk to someone trustworthy about it.**

## causes of depression

It is not fully understood why we develop depression, but genes or early life experiences may make some people more vulnerable. Life events that increase stress and physical illness may trigger an episode. In some people, it's not possible to easily identify a cause. Those with depression experience changes in the way the brain works—levels of stress chemicals are higher, and levels of "relaxing" chemicals lower.

## ways to lift depression

- **Try to keep as active as possible: exercise if you can manage it.**

- **Don't "drown your sorrows" with alcohol: it will make things worse.**

- **Beat insomnia: try the methods on page 96.**

- **Distract yourself: read, listen to the radio, speak to a good friend, watch a movie—whatever works best for you.**

- **Remember you are suffering an illness: you are not weak, and there are many thousands of other people going through a similar experience.**

# treatment options

Though you may not feel like it, getting treatment is vital. You might have to spell it out to your doctor, because many will not recognize "hidden" depression. A range of drug treatments and other therapies can be effective. Get informed by interrogating your doctor and joining internet support groups: with accurate information, you can help decide on the best choice of treatments.

## counseling

Many types of therapy are used to treat depression (see page 88). By talking it over, it's possible to recognize what triggers your depression symptoms before they occur. Some therapists will take you back to your past to look at the origins of your depression; others will concentrate more on the present.

## antidepressants

In working on levels of brain chemicals, these drugs treat the symptoms rather than the cause of the illness, but can be very useful in stabilizing emotions while you investigate the roots of the problem. Antidepressant drugs do not work immediately, but you should notice an effect after a few months. They will not change your personality, have few side-effects, and are not addictive.

right > **Exercise can be crucial to the ongoing management of depression, and allows you to stay motivated and positive. If nothing else, the routine of regular exercise is often reassuring.**

# coping with major illness

Having a major illness can be a devastating experience and is one of the chief causes of stress. Coming to terms with a significant health problem is a huge challenge, and you will experience a variety of emotions and feelings. You might have to make large and unforeseen adjustments to your way of living. There are good ways to help yourself cope—research your condition to the extent you want to, stay in touch with your feelings, get some support (including a good doctor), and make a plan for what to do if the situation gets worse.

Coming to terms with major illness is difficult. It is stressful to have to consider practical matters, such as finances, while worrying about the effects of your news on other people, and—perhaps the most complicated element—coming to terms with the emotional stages you will go through. There are some similarities with the levels of grief experienced by people after a loss (see page 142). At first, you may go into denial, thinking that this couldn't have happened to you. Next you will probably feel strong anger, then helplessness when you realize you can't instantly fix the situation. Then comes an overwhelming sadness that can cause apathy and loss of motivation. It also has the potential to trigger depression. Finally you will reach a level of acceptance, when the sadness begins to lift.

## benefits of support groups

• Opportunities to share feelings: others in a similar situation can help you talk about issues you might not want to discuss with family or friends.

• Insight, understanding, strength, and encouragement when it is lacking.

• Practical advice: people who've been in your position have a wealth of knowledge.

• Access to information: local, national, and international.

• Group activities: group relaxation or other stress-management techniques can be very comforting.

• Sense of belonging: offer the chance to meet new friends.

## work and money worries

The practicalities surrounding a major illness are likely to affect your finances. You might be unable to earn money, and may have to pay for some of your healthcare. Don't panic and take big decisions too quickly, but as soon as you feel able, make a financial plan to cover the situation. Bear in mind associated costs that might not be immediately obvious, such as paying someone to help with housework or look after your children. You might need professional financial help; if so, investigate whether you are entitled to free help before paying for an expert (see page 154). Find out also about any benefits you could apply for. If necessary, deal with the unpleasant step of making or updating your will.

Find out what your illness will mean in terms of your job, including how much sick or incapacity pay you will get and how long it will last for. If you think your employer might be treating you unfairly, take time to research your rights and then ask someone supportive to help you approach your manager.

below > **Group activities such as t'ai chi classes are often very reassuring in times of major illness.**

## positive coping strategies

- Get enough support: some people feel better being in charge of everything; others want someone else to take over. But everyone needs some form of emotional support.

- Learn about your illness: go slowly; if you overload yourself with information, you might have trouble taking it in, and feel overwhelmed and unable to cope. Make sure to use reliable sources, and stay optimistic. Note down questions to ask specialists and don't worry about taking up their time—your peace of mind is essential.

- Get recommendations about the best local specialist: try experts further afield if you are willing and able to travel. If your specialist makes you feel uncomfortable, take the matter into your own hands and change to another. The relationship between you and your doctor plays a significant role in the healing process.

## easing the effects on others

A health crisis causes a ripple effect that touches friends and relatives too. They may go through the same stages of acceptance and feel many of the same emotions as you do. Don't blame yourself for this, or feel guilty—it's hardly your fault. Allowing family and friends to become involved in a practical way could ease their worries. Don't take it personally if they get embarrassed and tongue-tied around you.

People may try to hide their feelings from you because they don't want you to have to

worry about them, so try to get them to open up so you can communicate effectively.

Be honest with others about your stage of recovery, even if they might be disappointed, and whatever you do, don't hide your illness through embarrassment—you'll be missing out on important understanding and support.

Notice the effects your illness is having on your close relationships, and keep lines of communication open. Your partner and children will probably be very fearful about the future, and dealing with it each in their own way. Encourage them to express their concerns with you or someone else they trust.

above > **Major illness often leads to feelings of isolation and even hostility to loved ones. But it is essential that you keep avenues of communication open and share your life and experiences with the people who care about you.**

# summary

- There are many on-the-spot techniques you can use when caught in an intensely stressful situation.

- Major life events happen to us all. Some are happy events that we choose; others we have no control over, but all bring a certain amount of stress and pressure.

- Help and advice is always available.

- Make it a priority to look after yourself by getting plenty of support. Above all, don't try to cope alone.

- Avoid trying to be perfect; nor should you expect other people and circumstances to be always as you would want them to be.

- Prepare for big events as much as possible beforehand.

- In your relationships, at work, and when managing money, develop strategies that lead to positive outcomes.

- Always get help when you experience severe physical and emotional symptoms.

- Find out what help is available—use your social network, books, and the internet.

# overview

I hope this book has given you a better understanding of what stress is, how it can affect you, and what you can do to manage it.

Remember it's your view of, and reactions to, an event that determine its impact. This means it's always possible to reduce the pressures you have to face. By knowing yourself well enough to tell when you're under stress you can take action to relieve the tension as soon as possible.

The time and effort you spend relaxing and learning new stress-management skills is always well spent because of the emotional and physical health benefits they bring. Let the skills you have learned guide you toward a healthy lifestyle in which you balance responsibilities with enjoyment. Surround yourself with close friends and family and enjoy the good times—they provide you with the strength to cope when life gets tough.

If you take just one thing away from reading this book, let it be an increase in the time you spend relaxing. This is the foundation upon which all other stress-management techniques are built. Without stopping for a few moments, it's impossible to gauge your current situation and frame of mind, and so gain insight into how you're being affected by events and what needs to change.

Managing stress takes life-long commitment—it's all too easy to slip back into bad habits. But notice how much better you feel and how much easier things are to deal with when you use positive strategies. This should convince you to keep it up if nothing else does. What at first feels like a tremendous effort soon becomes a habit that you don't even stop to think about.

Looking after yourself also has a beneficial effect on those close to you—you might get ill less often, and you'll probably be better company. They can learn from you how to achieve good balance in their own lives.

Effective stress management leads to a positive outlook on every aspect of life. Choose to take action against stress and you might find you have a better idea of what you want in life and a clearer idea of how to get it.

Above all, remember to look for the help you need when you are in trouble, and don't suffer in silence.

# professional support and advice (USA)

Below are just some of the biggest national organisations which can offer support and advice in difficult times. They can put you in touch with local resources in your area.

## Physical Health

- National Institutes of Health
  http://www.nih.gov
  health information and resources.

- Web MD
  http://www.webmd.com
  Wide range of information on healthcare.

## Mental Health

- National Hopeline Network
  1-800-784-2433/1-800-SUICIDE
  http://www.hopeline.com

- National Institute of Mental Health
  http://www.nimh.nih.gov

- National Mental Heath Association
  1-800-969-NMHA (6642)
  http://www.nmha.org

- National Foundation for Depressive Illness
  1-800-239-1265
  http://www.depression.org

- American Counseling Association
  1-800-347-6647
  http://www.counseling.org

## Parenting

- Research and Training Center on Family
  Support and Children's Mental Health
  1-503-725-4040
  http://www.rtc.pdx.edu

- Childhelp USA
  1-800-4-A-CHILD/1-800-422-4453
  http://www.childhelpusa.org

## Relationships

- American Association for Marriage and
  Family Therapy
  1-703-838-9808
  http://www.aamft.org

- National Coalition Against Domestic Violence
  1-800-799-SAFE (7233)
  http://www.ncadv.org

- National Resource Center on Domestic
  Violence
  1-888-Rx-ABUSE / 1-800-595-4889 (TDD)
  http://www.endabuse.org

- Rape, Abuse, and Incest National (RAIN)
  Network
  1-800-656-HOPE (4673)
  http://www.rainn.org

## Money

- The Motley Fool
  http://www.fool.com

- First Gov
  http://www.consumer.gov/yourmoney.htm

## Bereavement

- Compassionate Friends
  http://www.compassionatefriends.org

- AARP Grief and Loss
  http://www.aarp.org/griefandloss

- Survivors of Suicide
  http://www.survivorsofsuicide.com

- Rainbows International
  1-800-266-3206
  http://www.rainbows.org

You can find out what details are held about your credit history by contacting one of the three large national credit bureaus: Equifax, Experian, and Trans Union. You pay around $9 for a copy of your personal credit report, which can be ordered online. If the information on your file is incorrect, you can add a "statement of correction" of about 200 words, which will be given to lenders in the future.

# professional support and advice (UK)

Listed are some of the largest national organizations that can offer support and advice in difficult times. They can put you in touch with local resources in your area.

## physical health

- N.H.S. Direct
  0845 4647
  www.nhsdirect.nhs.uk

- Net Doctor
  www.netdoctor.co.uk

## mental health

- The Samaritans
  0845 790 9090
  www.samaritans.org

- Depression Alliance
  0845 123 2320
  www.depressionalliance.org

- The Mental Health Foundation
  020 7803 1100
  www.mentalhealth.org.uk

- British Association for Counselling and Psychotherapy (B.A.C.P.)
  0870 443 5252
  www.bacp.co.uk

- Alcoholics Anonymous
  0845 769 7555
  www.alcoholics-anonymous.org.uk

- Saneline
  0845 767 8000
  www.sane.org.uk

- Mind
  0845 766 0163
  www.mind.org.uk

- Association for Postnatal Illness
  020 7386 0868
  www.apni.org

## parenting

- Parentline Plus
  0808 800 2222
  www.parentlineplus.org.uk

- Fathers Direct
  0845 634 1328
  www.fathersdirect.com

- Working Families
  020 7253 7243
  www.workingfamilies.org.uk

- Gingerbread
  0800 018 4318
  www.gingerbread.org.uk

- Contact A Family
  0808 808 3555
  www.cafamily.org.uk

- Childcare Link
  0800 096 0296
  www.childcarelink.gov.uk

- Childline
  0800 1111
  www.childline.org.uk

- N.S.P.C.C.
  0808 800 5000
  www.nspcc.org.uk

- Supportline
  020 8554 9004
  www.supportline.org.uk

## relationships

- Relate
  0845 456 1310
  www.relate.org.uk
  Counseling by phone appointments
  0845 130 40.

## money

- Citizen's Advice Bureau (C.A.B.)
  020 7833 2181
  www.nacab.org.uk

- National Debtline
  0808 808 4000
  www.nationaldebtline.co.uk

- Job Centre Plus
  www.jobcentreplus.gov.uk

- Consumer Credit Counselling Service
  0800 138 1111
  www.cccs.co.uk

## bereavement

- Cruse Bereavement Care
  0870 167 1677
  www.crusebereavementcare.org.uk

- If I Should Die
  www.ifishoulddie.co.uk

## housing

- Shelter
  0808 800 4444
  www.shelternet.org.uk

# index

Page references in *italics* refer to captions.